Look at the Moon

A Mem.

Dad, Me, Mom

Suzi Schultz Gold

Copyright © 2020 Suzi Schultz Gold
All rights reserved.

Library of Congress Control Number: 2020905135

The events in this memoir are written based upon the author's memory. In many instances, the dialogue has been created to give the essence of the time and events.

The front cover illustration is taken from the announcement of the San Diego State College Commencement Exercises of June 13, 1941

A Tribute to Mom and Dad...

whose example of living a full and happy life still inspires me after more than seven decades. Without envy, always with a positive outlook and a sense of fairness, they lived each day by being mindful and grateful for their lot.

When the sun's first rays glimmer over the eastern horizon until the moon fades and those rays again bring light to a new day, I feel they are with me.

My Story

This is my story, simply one of luck. I am one of the fortunate ones. I was born in America, a country governed by a form of democracy, where power is given to the people and representatives of the people. Adding to my good fortune is that I was born in the mid 20th century, immediately after the most devastating war in history - especially for one of Jewish ethnicity.

In an egocentric way I wrote this for myself. Through these words I am able to travel back in time and relive a few of my most significant childhood memories. Months of writing and rewriting have turned to years. For each time I review an event that jogged a momentous recollection, I unearth a tiny detail that had been long buried by years of living.

I have discovered that each memory adds to my overflowing internal treasure chest. These tales from long ago are what I now value in my twilight years. When I am long gone and turn to dust who will have known my journey? Who will care? My wish is that sometime in the future a grandchild or a great great great grandchild will pick up my story, and want to discover their ancestors.

A safety net was always in place to catch me as I swung on a trapeze through youth, puberty, and adulthood. Team Charlotte and Sol, my Mom and Dad, allowed me to take risks, to fall and fail, always with the knowledge that they were there to catch me, to cheer me on, or help heal my wounds.

Each child in every family has a different relationship with his or her parents, recalling and viewing family history through different eyes. For perceptions are reality and this is mine.

I recognize that my narrative lacks drama. It is simply my journey guided by the two human beings who led by example. I am aware that my parents weren't perfect, but they were pretty close to it. They did their best! My tale is not filled with dirty laundry, just minor obstacles. During those times when there were options to consider Dad would say, "Make a decision. If it is the wrong one, forget it and make another one."

Most important, Mom and Dad bestowed on me the precious gift of unconditional love.

Mom & Dad
Charlotte & Sol Schultz

Table of Contents

Just to Bring a Smile

During the last few years of their lives, I spent an afternoon each weekend visiting my elderly parents. The time was special because it was mine, mine alone, although during the last couple of years "my" time was shared with a village of caregivers. My goal was to bring a smile and share a warm hug with Mom and Dad, offering a diversion to brighten their daily routine. But I also wanted to witness the caregivers, to confirm in my own mind that my folks were being well-cared-for. Was this merely a "job" for the rotating team of helpers? Did they feel any fondness for my dependent parents? Did they know how special and loved they were?

Mom and Dad still lived in the 2800+ square foot home in San Diego they had moved into when I left home for an out-of-state college in 1965. It was located on the crest of a hill straddled between the yacht filled San Diego Bay and the Pacific Ocean. When they first moved to Fleetridge, a newer area of Point Loma, one could get a glimpse of the bay beyond the floor to ceiling windows in their elegant living room with the blue-gray curved sofa and silk kelly green pillows. But the pine trees had matured over the years and the space was now filled with branches and tall shrubs. In reality, the view had become blocked by more than trees. The brightness was fading in their home. Darkness was edging in.

In contrast to my somber mood as I left my house, it was a glorious sunny Southern California Saturday afternoon. I backed down my driveway to begin the thirty mile drive south from my home in Poway, a north inland suburb of San Diego, to Mom and Dad's California ranch style home. I was operating on automatic as I approached the on-ramp to the freeway. I flipped on the radio to a station playing upbeat pop songs trying to counteract my sobering thoughts. As I followed the stream of cars ahead for the next forty minutes I tried, unsuccessfully, to mentally prepare for the challenging visit I knew was in store. I coached myself. *Think of all the wonderful family memories we have shared. Think of the full lives they have enjoyed. Be thankful they are here, that they have lived to reach old age. Just live in the moment. Just think about today.* But no matter how I struggled to lift my spirits, I knew reality would overtake my wishful sense of optimism.

I pulled up their steep driveway and turned off the motor as the radio died along with it. I sat absolutely still and stared at the home that held years of joyful family gatherings within the stucco walls. I took a deep breath. I already felt drained of energy, like all air had been sucked from my lungs. I wanted to climb down the rabbit hole and relive my world as it was years ago. But in real time I knew what I was facing and it wasn't the "good ole days." Today would be an instant replay of the past weekend, the past few weekends, really the past months.

My visits had become a depressing picture of old age. I never imagined this as the final chapter of my parents' story— an irreversible slippery slope eroding their quality of life. My visits were like a capsized ship with no hope of being turned upright, slowly sinking to the ocean floor. It was a dispiriting weekly event.

A small acknowledgment such as a smile or a hand reaching out to hold mine offered proof that Mom or Dad were still connected to life on earth. I thrived on those moments but hated that I clung to the tiniest of human actions and reactions.

When I unlatched the gate I thought about what I used to witness as I walked through the yard. I would be greeted with the shrill sound of a drill- *Zeh-Zeh-Zeh*-cutting through a sheet of Lucite in the garage. "Pop," the endearing name the grandkids had given Dad, had found a new hobby after retirement crafting photo frames, vases, or figurine stands, to give away.

Often I saw Pop tending to his beloved orchids in the garden. "Hey baby, what's new?" His blue eyes would sparkle when he saw me. With his hands covered by garden gloves and dirt, he would reach up from clipping and watering to kiss me on the cheek. But today there is no movement, no visible life in the yard as I walk to the back door.

To my right are dozens of cymbidium orchids in bloom. The exquisitely formed sprays of flowers: green, white, and pink, thrive on handmade platform benches Dad designed especially for their showy display.

I grasp the doorknob glancing at the dozens of decals Dad has placed above it, covering a large portion of the glass window in the door. These were mailed to him and showed support for everything from the San Diego Zoological Society to the Public Broadcasting Service to the United States Holocaust Museum to the U.S. Olympic Committee. His financial help crossed all lines of occupation, health, education, and diversity. I smile, remembering that he opened every single piece of mail addressed to Sol Schultz or "Occupant," including the stacks of solicitations from every 501c3 imaginable. When a dime was attached, when a few greeting cards were enclosed, when personalized address labels were included, Dad felt beholden to respond to the appeal with a few dollars. His generosity knew no borders. He was a lover of humanity.

I glance over the decals on the back window through the dust streaked glass as I prepare to enter the surreal. I see Mom and her caregiver at the kitchen table. I brace myself with forced cheerfulness. As I enter the kitchen a familiar smell hits my nostrils. It is a medicinal odor mixed with a musty sensation of the too warm airless house and of old age.

I don't see "my Mom," the energetic small package with the huge smile who for years cheerfully greeted me at the door. I ached to hear "Hi honey, I'm so glad to see you. Come see how the sweater I'm making you is coming along. How are the kids? What's Chuck doing today? How is work going?" I longed for the familiar fragrance of Elizabeth Taylor's signature perfume Dad bought her on every occasion.

In front of me is a frail woman trapped in a body that has become a curled and contracted shell. Mom now sits in a wheelchair, an oversized bib covering her torso, staring into space. Unable to feed herself, a caregiver is seated facing her, lifting a spoon filled with food to her lips. Most often the helpers give her food that she never enjoyed in her healthy years. She opens her mouth at the sight of the substance on the spoon. There is no delight in the taste or texture as the caregiver attempts to provide needed nourishment. One of the final joys of old age, the simple act of savoring the smell, taste, and texture of favored foods, is gone. Now Mom is sustained by thickened liquid and pureed meat. It is a conditioned response like Pavlov's dog. See the spoon, open your mouth.

Mom, who had applied tasteful, subtle, make-up to her fair skin for decades has a clownface on, adding to my sadness and despair. The caregivers have applied bold blue eye shadow across her eyelids and bright pink blush on her cheeks. One of the many lipsticks she collected through the years in a "free gift with purchase" promotion has been used to color her lips unevenly beyond her natural lip outline. She is dressed in loose unfashionable clothing that is easy to get on and off for she is incapable of completing this basic task without assistance. Her appearance with her hair freshly cut and dyed, her fingernails manicured, is a sad attempt to mask her failing mind.

"Hi Mom. I'm so happy to see you." I bend down to give her a side hug to avoid getting food on my clothes. The bib covering most of her unflattering top is covered with bits of food that have dropped out of her mouth. "Is your lunch good?" My cheerful voice defies my inner anguish. She glances my way with a dullness in her eyes and opens her mouth to speak. But her brain and voice cannot meaningfully connect and results in garbled sounds. "Ah-ah-ah-ga" on and on she struggles to express herself. The caregiver responds for her "Oh, she likes her lunch. See her smile?" Honestly, I see no visible pleasure in the blended food, and her "smile" is non-existent. The truth is that there is no acknowledgment that I am her daughter. Only I know that behind her vacant eyes is my treasured mother.

Dad is in his reclining chair half asleep. He prefers to doze in his chair since he can avoid the CPAP mask he has been prescribed to wear for sleep apnea. It is his way of bypassing the doctor's instructions. The mask resides safely next to his bed, unused, except at night.

The TV is on, as it is most days, with Dad's male caregiver entirely engrossed in *Wowowee*, a popular Filipino variety/comedy show. The staff taking care of Mom and Dad love this show, cheering the popular celebrity announcer and laughing along with the audience. I don't believe Dad understands the game but merely enjoys watching the caregivers' excitement. The continuous sound of the television is understandable. For the hours of boredom easily exceed the time necessary to ensure Mom and Dad are safe and taken care of.

I cross the room, acknowledging Tom, his large muscular caregiver, sitting nearby. I gently touch Dad on the arm. He glances my way, opens his eyes a sliver, and I give him a hug. It is up to me to initiate the kiss on the cheek. "Hi Poppy, how are you feeling?" He opens his eyes wider, gives me a smile of recognition, "Pretty good today baby." He turns away and refocuses on the TV screen. Though his mind at ninety-two is relatively sharp, his body has physically declined, betraying him. Age has robbed him of his interest in anything outside of the four walls. The days of asking about my life are over. His world has closed in. But he is comfortable at home, with a village to help him navigate through the daily struggles so often taken for granted.

The compact powerful man that he once was cannot raise himself to stand anymore. His legs have no strength though he retains a will that defies his body. "Tom" he calls out, "I need to go to the bathroom." Tom, a tall man in his mid-forties moves up to the reclining chair. He uses his strength to pull Dad upright from the motorized lounge chair where he is almost vertical. He rolls the wheelchair close, lifts and turns Dad ninety degrees, and gently places him in the wheelchair. Julie, another caregiver, follows behind, ready to assist in helping Dad sit on the toilet. "Julie doesn't mind doing this. She likes to look at my ass," Dad jokes on the ride to the bathroom. A few minutes later, with clothing back in place and hands washed, Tom places his strong arms under Dad, and carefully lifts him and sets him back in the wheelchair. He pushes him down the hall, back to the recliner and transitions him once again into a comfortable position. Dad lets out a long sigh as he settles in to stare at the TV screen.

I keep reminding myself that these are the choices he has insisted on for his remaining years. "Mom and I want to stay at home, in our house, no matter what." I am in my mid 60's and question, *Is this really the best place for them to be? Is this what I would want?* But it is not my decision. It is not my life. It is theirs.

Mom has been rolled in her wheelchair back to the bedroom for a rest. She has been lifted onto the spacious king-size bed that dwarfs her small frame. She has slept in this bed beside Dad for decades though now the scene has changed. Pillows have been placed around her and a three foot side rail has been positioned between the box spring and mattress to prevent her from falling onto the floor. On Dad's side, the CPAP machine sits on the nightstand, water still remaining in it from the previous night.

For the next couple of hours I rotate between the family room and the bedroom in a one-way conversation doing my best to generate a spark in either Mom or Dad. I spend a few minutes rambling to Mom with no effect: no facial expressions, gestures, or response. "Mom, I heard from Josh this week. It's snowing in New York. I can't believe my California kid likes the snow and the east coast. Lindsay is doing great at her job. She takes care of Veterans now." On and on I chatter—about my work, about the weather, about anything and everything.

I switch gears and converse with one of the women hovering near me. "How is she doing? Is she sleeping okay? Has she shown any awareness?" The caregivers know how to respond. "Look how happy she is. She likes us to comb her hair and paint her nails so she looks pretty." I nod. *Really? Who are you kidding?* Though I am appreciative of the care that Mom is receiving, I am somewhat resentful of the intimacy these women seem to feel towards my mother. They treat her like a child, unaware that trapped inside her body is my smart, kind, loving, mother. I want to ask them to leave the room and give me private time with her, but I can't bring myself to do this knowing that I will be depending on their care and leaving in a short time for another week. I feel somewhat angry, yet resigned. I certainly don't have the patience to take care of my parents 24/7 no matter how deep my love is. So I grin and bear it.

I sit next to Dad on the sofa and tell him about my week at work, trying to keep a conversation going. "Pop, have you watched any good movies on TV this week? Have you gone to Sammy's for lunch in the last few days? Did you watch the football game last week? How are the Chargers doing?" I continue the questions in an attempt to spark interest. He answers simply with a "yep," "sure," "no," and does not encourage communication. It is a one-way street. Inside my heart breaks. I want to run away. I want to take the years back and freeze the time when our family shared a closeness. I miss the interaction, the enthusiasm and joy that overflowed from my parents when family members were in their presence. I miss their perpetual interest in my life. Our roles have changed.

I walk down the narrow hall to the bedroom and lean over the bed rail to reach Mom. She turns her head towards me as my lips brush her cheek. She has a look of confusion as if she is wondering, "Who is that person?" I head back to Dad's recliner and give him a hug and kiss good-bye. "I'll see you in a few days, Pop," I remind him. He barely glances my way, one eye on the TV. "Love you baby" his soft voice rings. I say a silent prayer of thanks and rejoice in the fact that my folks are still here.

I back out of the driveway heading home with tear-filled eyes. I hang close to the slow lane as my mind wanders reviewing the few positive seconds of the visit, but I am virtually in another place. I am a horse heading back to the stable, to the safe haven of my own home. I attempt to dig deep into my thoughts to appraise, validate, then reconcile this inevitable circle of life, focusing on lives well lived. Though Mom and Dad can no longer verbalize or display their emotions, it does not matter. I make this weekly visit selfishly. I only need to see them and to give them a hug. I still know their love exists somewhere within their declining bodies.

I have come to understand that the importance is in remembering each step of the journey to the summit of life, as well as the painful lessons of the path traveled back down.

Broken Mold

"Enough is enough. Fair is fair!" His voice bellowed and he paced the family room as he shouted to the recipient of his fury on the telephone. "Bernie, what are you trying to do? Screw me?" Then after a brief lull of audible conversation, his voice dropped decibels and his tone became friendly. "Okay, that sounds fair enough. Let's do it. We'll talk later," he responded with a cheerful lilt. He walked the coiled cord back across the room and placed the telephone in its cradle. Then he turned, spying me in the room. "Hi, Peanut, whatcha doing?" His smile was wide, showing the gold crown covering his molar on the left side of his mouth that was only visible with his grin. Suddenly, without hesitation, all memory of his ire had dissipated.

That was my dad, Sol Schultz. His range of emotions switched with lightning speed from exasperation to compromise. In the blink of an eye his voice became calm and he moved on. You always knew where you stood and what was on his mind.

I am convinced his make-up was 75% sugar and 25% a blend of spices including: the earthiness of Cumin, the nuttiness of Poppy Seeds, the sweet woody flavor of Cinnamon, and the hotness of Pepper. Yes, along with an abundant sense of humor, he did have a short fuse. His fury and fire would flare up then extinguish itself, often immediately after the message had found the target. The lightness in his voice would return while the recipient of his anger was beginning to grasp the significance of the message. To say he was unique does not do Dad justice. I am convinced my dad was one of a kind.

I'm not citing the "Father Knows Best" dad who arrives home in a suit after a long day at the office, gives his wife a peck, gives his kids a quick hug, sits in his easy chair in front of the TV and waits for a drink, the aroma of a hot meal permeating from the kitchen. That was the TV dad of the sixties.

I'm not referring to today's dad: the soccer coach, the weekend dad, the stay-at-home dad with the working wife, or the "give 'em a bath, read 'em a story, put 'em to bed" dad.

My dad, with his stocky build on his 5'7" frame, had a wavy head of brown hair framing his receding hairline, and light blue eyes. He used to joke about my short stocky frame. "You look like a Russian shot putter" he would say. I took no offense by this comment. To me, it meant that I took after him and that was fine, thick thighs and all.

His mantra, long before it was used by Nike, was "Just do it." His entrepreneurial spirit led him to explore multiple vocations and careers. He tried teaching, real estate, retail, wholesale, liquidation, and was an amateur inventor and writer. Dad was a forward thinker, but not particularly adventurous or worldly. He loved a challenge and was a calculated risk taker in business. He was a contradiction; an extrovert who never met a stranger yet was shy at the same time. He was a lover of people, a lover of life, and had a love of comedy.

He trusted everyone and negotiated with humor and fairness. Dad saw "people" – not color, religion, ethnicity, size, or age. The one area where Dad had monovision was in regards to the love of his life. Mom, his college sweetheart, was his first and only love. His romanticism stopped at Mom. He was not a Casanova. He even balked at dancing with anyone but her. When she was asked to dance by another man at a party she encouraged Dad to take a turn with her partner's spouse. "Sol, it's rude not to ask her to dance, even if you don't want to." She would mention it on the ride home in anticipation of the next occasion when the situation might arise. Sometimes he would reluctantly comply. Other times he would make a dash for the food table to avoid a swing on the dance floor with anyone other than Mom. The timid man with the perennial smile and boundless energy was my dad. I believe that mold simply crumbled after my dad made his debut.

Chief Happiness Officer

Mom, born Charlotte Joy Fried, was our North Star. She watched over the family with tenacity; ready to listen and to provide guidance and direction. She was small in height, with womanly curves in her slim figure and an oversized brain. She was the perennial optimist.

After she passed away I often heard her friends comment "Your sweet mother was the smartest person I knew." She was a voracious reader, extremely interested in politics, was the ultimate liberal thinker, and was always in the corner of social justice. When Mom was in high school her teacher informed her that she was getting a "C" on her report card. The teacher explained, "Charlotte, I know you have a high IQ. I read in your file that your IQ is 144. You just aren't applying yourself. I know you are capable of much better work. I am giving you an average grade because that is how you are performing."

Mom's intellectual ability wasn't particularly important to me in my youth. I appreciated everything else about her. She possessed quiet strength, creativity, an unequaled love of family, and a generous nature. She was the CHO of our family, Chief Happiness Officer, and it was a full time job. She was a Pollyanna, the peacemaker, the ambassador and diplomat to ten people that made up our family. Her salary through the years was paid in time spent together with children and grandchildren, and she felt wealthy. Her bonuses could be measured in our closeness as a family. She had the ability to see her glass as half full, to be positive and look on the bright side of every situation. Her values were in the right order…'family first' and 'we have everything we need'.

Monday through Friday I walked the two blocks from my elementary school so I could eat my lunch at home. Mom made sure she was there to give me a loving hug and a tuna sandwich.

This special time was mine alone with Mom. It must have stifled her social life: her card games, errands, luncheons, and volunteer work. But she never complained. I was her daughter, and she was my security blanket. I took it for granted that she would always be home for me at lunchtime.

1

Grandma & Grandpa Schultz: Immigrants

"Give me your tired, your poor,
your huddled masses yearning to breathe free..."
Emma Lazarus

Other than those of Native American ancestry, all United States citizens can discover immigrants in their family history. Whether they came in prosperity or despair, by choice or by force, between 1880 and 1920 America received more than twenty million immigrants. The majority of arrivals came from Central, Eastern and Southern Europe and were of many nationalities and religions. Jews from Eastern Europe were most often fleeing religious persecution. The blend of diverse cultures created a melting pot. Immigration was the story of America.

Grandpa, Lazarus Schultz, was born on November 20, 1877 in Sasoff, Austria. He was 5' 6 3/4" and 150 lbs. with a fair complexion, almost transparent blue eyes, and an identifying mole on the right side of his forehead. My grandmother, Anna Woolf, was born on February 11, 1880 in Tarnow, Austria. Her dark eyes were penetrating, made more piercing with her hair pulled back into a bun. Grandpa would refer to their birthplace as "Galicia" since the land that was previously part of Poland had been annexed by the Habsburg Empire and became part of the Austro-Hungarian Empire from 1867-1918. The country changed hands with each war, so their mother country was determined wherever the border happened to be following a conflict.

Lazarus and Anna met and courted in their homeland, speaking mostly Yiddish, a German language mixed with Hebrew words. Yiddish, unquestionably, is the world's most expressive language. Common Yiddish words used today, such as "schmuck," "chutzpah," and "mensch," are so visual, so full of passion, that it is hard to translate them with adequate expression. They are often best defined through hand gestures and voice inflection. Though the couple communicated to each other in this language, they realized it was necessary to learn English when they made the decision to depart Austria.

Anna's sister, Becky, had immigrated to England. Becky's letters describing life in Britain encouraged Anna to leave Austria and join her sister in Manchester, England. Whether the attraction was the stable government, potential job opportunities, or the prospect that life had to be better, Anna was enticed to leave Austria for England.

Lazarus stayed behind, seeking the necessary financial means and documents to emigrate. He was only afforded a second grade education but his street skills combined with a fearless restlessness gave him confidence beyond his formal schooling.

He approached a scholarly friend, "Kensta helpin?" This translated in English means "Can you help me?" His friend agreed to write a letter giving him permission to depart Austria. The letter was written in Yiddish which he passed off to the border guards as a permit to leave the town. The guards at the border crossing couldn't read Yiddish so Lazarus explained, "...a letter from the Mayor permitting me to exit." His hometown was so small it was without a photographer or official to stamp permits so official letters were the passports, visas, or what have you. The guards studied the words as they attempted to interpret the Yiddish. They huddled together speaking in whispers. Finally, resigned, the guard waved his arm across his body impatiently and declared, "Mache weiter,"(Go on.) Apparently, his story was plausible enough, or the guards were apathetic enough, that he was able to pass through western Europe to join Anna.

Lazarus found passage to England, where the reunited couple proceeded to marry in London in November 1901. Though the immigrants faced many obstacles: foreign language, unfamiliar customs, a different currency, and strange social expectations, all were deemed preferable to the challenges they faced in their prior life. They only hoped that "the streets of England were paved with gold," or at least paved. They settled in the bustling city of Manchester and their firstborn daughter, Lillian, arrived in September 1902.

Like many immigrants, Lazarus sought work as a peddler. He was given a Pedlar's Certificate from the City of Manchester authorizing him to act as a peddler within any part of the United Kingdom.

Before long, Becky again forged west. She had attained a visa permitting her to immigrate to America, the place that promised to be the land of opportunity. She settled in St. Louis, Missouri, the fourth largest city in the United States at the time.

In 1880 the Jewish community of St. Louis numbered 10,000 out of 350,000 people. They were mostly German immigrants. Embracing life and prospering in America, Becky sent letters to the family in England encouraging them again to join her and volunteering to sponsor them.

Dreams of prosperity crossed the Atlantic in record speed and provided the bait and courage for Anna and Lazarus to consider the long daunting journey. So, in 1904, a few months before the birth of son Jack, Lazarus packed his worldly goods in a cardboard leather-strapped trunk. He left by himself on a ship from Liverpool, entering the United States at Port Huron, Michigan on December 15, 1903. "I'll send for you and the children as soon as I get the money needed for passage," he told Anna.

"You see, ven I got off de boat in America and vent to de desk, the person sitting there just ask me my name and wrote it however he thought right. He wrote S-c-h-u-l-t-z." This story was passed on, though a different spelling of his surname was never confirmed. In an attempt to fit into this adopted land, Lazarus of Galicia became Louis of America.

Louis found employment in a ladies' cloak factory as a tailor. The owner took a liking to him and offered to promote him. "Louis, I would like you to become my foreman. I think you would do a good job. What do you think?" Louis declined. "It's okay but no. I am happy vere I am." Most likely, this was because he could neither read nor write English.

By August of 1905 Louis had accumulated enough money to send for his family in England. He prepared for the arrival of his wife, Anna, 25 years old, and their two children. Anna arrived by ship on the east coast, docking in Philadelphia, Pennsylvania. Louis was excited to reunite with his family. Ten months later a third child, a daughter they named Ida, was born in June 1906, her birthright making her a U.S. citizen. For the next ten years the Schultz family adjusted to living in St. Louis, striving to succeed in America.

In 1916, David Gershon, a friend originally from Galicia, wrote a letter to Louis about San Diego, California. "You wouldn't believe it. The city has a glorious harbor and the weather is the same everyday, mild and sunny." The country's seventh largest city boasted a population of more than 74,000 in 1920. The center of the city was filled with shops and boarding houses and a military presence was growing significantly.

Sprinkled in the mix of California's southern city was a tiny Jewish population reputed to be somewhere between 110 and 2,000, as the actual number cannot be confirmed. "Jewish geography" was common. Every Jewish family knew every other Jewish family or was acquainted with someone who knew that family or at least knew some gossip about them.

So Louis and Anna packed up their three children and their worldly goods for the third time. The hope that the grass was even greener in California was the impetus that drove Louis to leave relatives in Missouri. Upon arrival, the Schultz family searched for housing in the hub of the city. They found a suitable boarding house in downtown San Diego where an unexpected surprise was in store for the family of five.

2

Surprise!

"Mein Gott. How can this be?" Anna exclaimed when she found herself pregnant a fourth time at the age of 38. No one in the household, adult or child, was excited about the addition of a baby to the family. Anna expressed her concern. "I got three children already. Ve have more than enough mouths to feed." As the months passed, though with a lack of enthusiasm, Anna and Louis prepared for the reality that the family would squeeze yet another human being into their tight living space.

Nearby, on 30th and B Street, Dr. Dail's Maternity Hospital was located. It was established in 1909 serving the community with a total of ten beds. On May 27, 1918, my dad, Solomon Schultz, entered the world at Dr. Dail's, bellowing to his mother and anyone else who was within earshot. Being the fourth child of Anna and Louis Schultz, and not necessarily one anxiously or joyously anticipated, the small fair-haired bundle immediately made his presence known. Anna had no trouble expressing her feelings about this package of wails.

After first laying eyes on her baby boy, Anna was rumored to express herself openly and loudly. She slapped her palm against her forehead and shouted "THASALL." The nurses were convinced that Anna had decided on the baby's name by yelling out "That's Sol!" Thus, his birth certificate states

'Solomon Schultz" and no middle name was ever added.

Within the family there was discord with the birth of baby Sol. Dad's two sisters and one brother were unhappy that their physical space would be cramped even more. Plus, they were truthfully mortified that their mother had given birth so late in life

Dad's oldest sibling, Lil, was 16 years old and a student at San Diego High School when Dad was born in 1918. One month after Dad's birth the San Diego Union newspaper covered a student strike at San Diego High School. The article began "Politics and education mixed poorly in the spring of 1918 when the San Diego Board of Education abruptly fired nineteen teachers at San Diego High School. The action would lead to a mass walkout of students from the school and local newspaper headlines rivaled news of the war in Europe." This was sister Lil's senior year and she joined the student walkout. The standoff event was all the encouragement Lil needed to leave school forever and go out on her own. She left San Diego with a girlfriend and moved one hundred miles north to Los Angeles. The end of her education could be blamed on the school strike and possibly a little on her new baby brother. In a short time Lil fell in love and a few years later married Ted, a dental supply salesman.

Baby Sol was unaware of the tumultuous times in which he was born. Six months after his birth, in November of 1918, after the long four years and thirteen days of the first World War, the Treaty of Versailles was signed. Somewhere between nine and thirteen million lives had been claimed during the Great War.

A couple of weeks before that historic date an influenza outbreak spread throughout the world. "Spanish Flu" infected a billion people and killed as many as fifty million. It was one of the deadliest pandemics in history. In San Diego that year there were 4,392 cases and 324 people died of the flu. Children chanted this rhyme in 1918 while skipping rope.

I had a little bird

Its name was Enza

I opened the window

And in-flew-enza

When the disease struck San Diego, the city's Board of Health urged the public to "keep out of crowds." As a precautionary measure, the City Council ordered the closure of all indoor public places. Theaters, moving picture shows, churches, dance halls, schools, and libraries were closed. Fortunately, the Schultz family escaped the illness. They went about their daily lives in the center of downtown, though the flu caused a significant fear throughout the city.

Louis found work that didn't require literacy, just manual labor. He woke up daily before the sun rose to set up a stand and sell produce at the local market. He worked long hours arranging the vegetables and fruit in order to support his wife and children. The long hours and drudge of work often ended in an evening of alcohol and cards.

From 1920-1933, much to Louis' dismay, prohibition in the United States covered a nationwide constitutional ban on the production, importation, transportation, and sale of alcoholic beverages.

Louis had rented five rooms downstairs in a boarding house at 1013 F Street, each with an outside entrance. Even with Lil no longer living in San Diego, the rooms including a kitchen, eating area, and living room, were crowded for five people. Anna creatively blocked all except one of the outside entrances with furniture. A sewing machine blocked one door and that room was also used as a dining room. A trunk that had traveled across the ocean secured the door to Dad's father and brother's bedroom. Another trunk was placed in front of the door to the "little bedroom" which Dad shared with his mother. Sister Ida slept in the front room on a nice metal bed.

The kitchen had a single cold water faucet and a tea kettle was always heating water on the gas stove. The area opened to the back porch where a galvanized laundry tub stood and was filled with the hot water for weekly baths. The tub had multiple purposes in that it was shared by the family for face washing, hand washing, and shaving. As a small child Dad bent his growing body each week like a pretzel to squeeze himself in to the soothing warmth of the heated water.

After his bath, Dad would run to his mother shivering, "Ma, Ma, Ma, warm me, warm me." His mother would wrap him up in a sheet and he would jump under the huge down comforter that his father had carried over from England. There were two ways to get warm on a cold night. With teeth chattering, the curly haired boy would snuggle under the huge feather bedcovers or stand by the three burner stove.

Dad at Lincoln Elementary School

Bathing in the laundry tub was a family event for Dad until he had grown too large for the tub. He then joined his friends in the neighborhood who were going to the "Y" for showers. The cost was five cents, providing you brought your own towel. He did this for four years, every Saturday and also on the Jewish High

9

Holidays. One Saturday when he went to Olson's grocery store with his mother, Mrs. Olson smiled, "My, doesn't Solly look nice." His hair was slicked with Pomade Vaseline and he was feeling very dapper. "Yes, he just came from the "Y" where he showered," Anna announced proudly. "Oh," said Mrs. Olson, "I didn't know Solly was a member of the Young Men's Christian Association." That was the end of showers at the YMCA.

From that day on, Louis took Dad to the bathhouse. Salt water was pumped from the bay and heated. Special soap was needed to lather. Bathing culminated in rinsing in cold water. The total cost of the bath and soap was $0.25.

The place that accommodated San Diego's dirtiest from 1920 is today the location of San Diego's Convention Center built in 1989. It is constructed in a unique multipurpose design, one that does not include a bathhouse.

The single toilet shared by all family members was located on the back porch, making it a challenge to use during the darkness of night without waking up others. The lack of an indoor toilet became an embarrassment to Dad as he grew older.

The living quarters were a single wall construction, tongue and groove, which Louis had wallpapered in the popular tradition of classy homes of the day. Being somewhat of a hyperactive kid, Dad found great pleasure in running his finger down the joints and splitting the paper. "Solly, vat are you doink? Stop it," Louis would shout. "I can't spend $25 every year to have the house repapered."

Upstairs, above the Schultz family, lived five individual roomers. The walls of the boarding house lacked insulation and the wood and linoleum flooring provided no sound buffer. The sound of roomers above walking around and the repetition and groans of a rocking chair drove the family wild: *cre-e-a-ak, sq-q-squeak, cre-e-a-a-k*. When it became unbearable, Louis or

Anna took the broom handle and poked it a few times with a *thump, th-ump, th-ump,* on the ceiling to quiet the neighbors, saying under their breath in Yiddish "Zol zine shah! Ich ben meshuga." (Be quiet. I am going mad.) The noise didn't abate nor did the complaints about the neighbors.

Safety with regards to electricity was never a concern. Throughout the house there was a double socket, plus a double socket, plus a double socket attached by cords to the light cord hanging in the center of the rooms. There was no wall outlet, just the two strands of wires along the ceiling separated by porcelain dividers and a single drop light in each room. In order to read in bed, Dad used the extra extension to light the pages.

Refrigerators were becoming popular but were too costly for the Schultz family. Their kitchen was equipped with an icebox, a common standard of the day. The iceman would deliver a block of ice on a regular basis to the boarders. The ice was placed in the top compartment in a tray with a drip pan underneath to catch the water. Sometimes the drip pan overflowed and the room had to be mopped up. This task was easily accomplished because of the linoleum floors.

Opposite the home was the grocery store. Adolf, Emma, and Claus Spreckels, a prominent real estate family who founded the Spreckels Sugar Company, owned the property and had reconfigured two rooms into a grocery store with three rooms for living purposes. Mr. and Mrs. Olson operated the market. Typical of small stores at the time, most customers used a charge account. Accounts were to be paid up monthly and high prices made up for the late payments.

Ice cream was one of the most popular items and was scooped from a non-electric freezer. This was actually a wooden case where the ice cream was delivered in metal containers and packed with ice and rock salt then tramped down with what looked like a wooden pick. The ice cream delivery man filled it with ice and salt once a week. The Olsons always carried two flavors, vanilla and maple nut. On delivery day Dad knew to hang around the grocery store when the metal containers were replaced. Then he would sweetly sidle up, "Hi Mrs. Olson. Got any leftover ice cream?" It was a lucky day when he got a scoop.

Dad bought one cent candies as often as he had a bit of change. He loved the sweets and paid handsomely for this indulgence. When he was twelve years old his mother took him to his first dental appointment, resulting in two rotten teeth having to be pulled.

Anna bought milk, cream, and white bread at the Olson's store but meat and poultry were purchased at a kosher butcher in accordance with Jewish tradition and laws. Kosher chickens, slaughtered in a way to cause little trauma to the chicken, are soaked and salted, de-feathered in cold water, and then certified by a rabbi.

Chicken soup, often called the "Jewish Penicillin", was a staple in many Jewish households. In the Schultz house the poultry was not a medical panacea but a weekly over-boiled, tasteless, fall off the bone, chicken. Dad summed up his mother's cooking. "Ma was ahead of her time practicing Cajun style cooking. Everything that wasn't boiled was burned. We didn't need an alarm clock in our house. Every morning I woke up to the sound of a knife scraping the burnt crumbs off the surface of the toast." This was most likely responsible for Dad's lifetime dislike of chicken.

On April 22, 1932 in the Superior Court of San Diego, California, Lazarus Schultz, now known as Louis, raised his right hand to "renounce allegiance to any foreign prince..." His race was listed on the Declaration of Intention as "Hebrew."

He now had a homeland whose borders were solid. He was 54 years old, having traveled from Europe to England to America. He was now a United States citizen.

* * * * *

Grandpa Schultz Becomes a U.S. Citizen

3

"Be Careful Crossing De Street"

Dad's brother, Jack, was fourteen years older and had quit school at thirteen years of age. Jack was a good-looking, street savvy kid, with a full head of black hair. He had a bike, enabling him to get a job working as a delivery boy for Western Union. Being a teen with a job allowed Jack to be out of the house a good deal of the time.

After two years of biking to deliver telegrams, he had saved enough money by the age of sixteen to buy a Ford. Owning a car opened up a new opportunity for Jack as he considered an offer from his dad. "Jack, how 'bout you come to work the produce market with me? I could use help. With the car you make deliveries to the customers." This was an improvement over biking telegrams around town and Jack agreed.

Dad often went with his big brother to help pack and carry the fruits and vegetables. His payment was his favorite; an Eskimo Pie ice cream bar. One day Dad accompanied Jack on a delivery, anticipating the delicious chocolate covered ice cream bar. "Jaaaaaack, I want my ice cream," Dad tugged on Jack's jacket. "Later, Sol. We have to make some deliveries first." "Jaaaack, I want my ice cream now," Dad whined. Jack ignored his little brother. Sulking, Dad sat in the car refusing to help his brother get the fruits and vegetables sorted and boxed.

Ten minutes later he calmed down and his mood improved. He gathered a package of vegetables and left the car. A minute after he exited the vehicle, a drunk driver rammed into the Ford and totaled it. Jack and his customer heard the crash and jumped into another car. They chased the intoxicated man who was making a quick getaway. They quickly overtook him, pinned him down and held him until the police arrived. Dad was left alone crying, but was easily pacified by a lady who bought him some milk and cookies. He would get an Eskimo Pie next trip.

At five years of age, Dad was old enough to begin his education as a kindergartener at Lincoln Elementary School. In September 1923, his mother opened the door of the boarding house and pointed for the small boy to leave. Dad was not at all prepared. He wasn't quite sure how to get to school or what to expect when he arrived there. As he cautiously headed down the steps to the sidewalk, he turned back to glance at his ma.

Anna was older than most mothers with a young child. Her hair had streaks of gray and frizzy strands framed her face. Her thick arms were crossed in front of her, resting on the printed housedress that draped around her short but ample frame. The sturdy black shoes she wore were sensible wear for immigrants accustomed to carrying bags of food from the market to home, as she had on the cobblestone streets of her previous villages. Anna's manner and appearance were the same as when she had come across the ocean a few years prior with a worn trunk, the clothes on her back, and hope.

She stood at the landing of the boarding house. Her small curlyheaded boy yearned to turn back, to reach for the security of his mother's fleshy hand for protection against the unknown. "Ma, do I go straight?" She motioned with her hand waving. "Geyn, geyn (Go, go)-Straight down de street to de school." In a heavy accented voice she concluded "Be careful crossing de street -Geyn."

To Anna, who was unaware of American norms, it seemed natural to send your child off to public school by himself. Dad proceeded to walk the few blocks to begin his formal education. He looked both ways before crossing the street as his mother had told him. His blond hair and light freckles across the bridge of his nose gave him an innocent appearance. Dad looked straight ahead, unsure of what he would encounter, but full of curiosity.

He approached the schoolyard and stepped up to the desk in the auditorium to ask how to get to Kindergarten.

"Hello, what is your name, little man?" the smiling woman sitting behind the desk glanced to the right then the left.

"I'm Solly Schultz," he replied in a strong voice.

"Where is your mother?"

"Oh, she's at home fixing the house. She sent me here to go to school."

"Where's your father?"

"Oh, he's working in the market."

"I see," the young woman's eyebrows lifted. "You will need to fill out this form. Can you do that?"

Dad took the paper in his stubby little fingers. He was quiet as he looked it over. He tried to figure out the jumbled letters. He took a deep breath.

"I can't. I don't know what it says." Even for a kid with lots of gumption, this was asking too much. Dad's bottom lip quivered. "Don't worry, I'll help you. You just tell me your name again and I will do the writing," the kind lady replied in a soft voice. "I'm Solly, Solly Schultz." He recited his address as he had practiced, and his parents' names. The rest of the registration form was left blank. And Dad went off to Room 1 as directed.

There was only one kindergarten class and Dad was eager to please. When his teacher asked, "Who will help move the tables and chairs into a circle?" "I will," Dad volunteered. In fact, he volunteered to do anything that needed to be done. When it was time for music, Dad raised his hand as high as he could, hoping to be picked to play one of the instruments. He was proud to be chosen to play the triangle in the band, using a little wooden stick.

He loved the extra activities during school, particularly physical education. The highlight of each day was recess where he played kickball on the playground. By the end of second grade he knew his way around the school, inside the classroom and on the playground. He even got a taste of politics in an upper grade, serving as president of the school for one month.

Academics were not the focus of Dad's education and his grades resembled a line graph appearing like a mountain range of highs and lows. But his folks were not familiar with the schools or the grading system in America so Dad allegedly was able to capitalize on their lack of knowledge.

He brought his report card home, presented it to his parents and proudly declared, "Take a look at my good grades." Most grades fell in the middle of the grading curve. He announced that "F" stood for "fine" and "A" meant "awful." His mom grinned widely. "So vat you think of mine Solly?" Anna crowed to the neighbors about the report card. "He's de smartest one in de femly." Dad had earned high marks for creativity. As he was promoted to the upper grades, his grades thankfully improved. The wheels of his mind were constantly working and he found a way to reinterpret his report card favorably to his folks.

Even at a young age Dad showed an interest in creative writing. He had a flair for short stories and poems. His first published poem was in Lincoln Memories in June 1930. He was twelve years old and graduating to junior high from

Lincoln Elementary School.

DAYS AT LINCOLN

Days at Lincoln will soon be done,

To other children, their days just begun

But to us who are going away,

We look at promotion another way

Don't forget your days at Lincoln

Let your loyal hearts be one,

To love, live and be honest each day,

To think of Lincoln in every way.

His student prophesy at graduation from Lincoln Elementary School was to be a "Raiser of vegetables without seeds." While he succeeded in many things, this was not one of them.

At nineteen years old, brother Jack went to work for a slot machine company and was put in charge of the casino slots twenty-six miles across the sea from the California coast on Catalina Island. Catalina was a popular destination. It was close by and offered legalized gambling. Jack became an expert in repairing the slot machines, ensuring the bells and sirens would trigger and coins would drop into the cup as jackpots were hit.

Within a few years Jack moved back to San Diego and married his girlfriend Ruby who was from Eureka, California. "Ruby is such a nice girl," his father, Louis, told Jack. He was especially pleased when Jack added, "She has converted. She is now Jewish." Though this was never confirmed, it pleased Louis and Anna.

Ida, Dad's closest sibling in age, was twelve years Dad's senior and his delegated babysitter. She quit school in junior high to help her mother with the household chores.

Dad was five years old when, at 17, Ida met a sweet, handsome young man named Jimmy Wilson, who sold produce for Louis. Though he was a hard worker, Jimmy had two strikes against him in Louis' eyes. "They's just children and he's not a Jew. Vat is she thinking?" Louis fumed to Anna. Their despair had no effect, and Jimmy and Ida ran off and eloped. Louis and Anna were furious. Anna's resolve softened in due time and was somewhat forgiving, but for years Louis would turn his head away from Ida as if she were invisible. There was an equal amount of thawing time before he would speak to Jimmy. The birth of their only child, a daughter Betty Jean, helped to warm the relationship.

By the time Dad was in elementary school all three siblings had moved out of the family home pursuing their own paths. Due to vast age differences, Dad hardly knew his siblings. He lived with his parents almost as an only child.

Dad was certain that his mother and father never slept together after he was born, possibly to prevent another accident. All arguments between his mother and father were in spoken in Yiddish so he had no idea what they were saying or arguing about —but he figured it was most likely about him.

4

Finding the Way Home

The Rose Park Playground, located at 11th and I Street, became Dad's after school haven when he was about nine years old. He walked home after school then headed to the playground until it closed. Then he proceeded up 2nd Street past the produce markets that were open well into the night, where vendors were sorting, restocking and rearranging vegetables and fruit for display. He followed the road home from the market to 10th and F Street.

On rainy days he went to the Children's Library that was open until 9:00 in the evening at 8th and A Street and read. Dad was an avid reader of fiction. He devoured sports books and juvenile books by American writer Clarence Buddington Kelland. Kelland wrote the Mark Tidd series about an overweight stutterer who, with a few friends, got the better of potential bullies. Dad loved the adventures and antics of the characters, though research regarding Kelland suggests that his stories would be politically controversial today.

Following the traditions of Orthodox Judaism, the family joined Tifereth Israel Synagogue located at 18th and Market Street. Each week Dad walked to the synagogue for Hebrew School after public school. A photo of Dad at 13 years of age, complete with tallit and yarmulke, a prayer shawl and skullcap, shows

Rabbi Firestone and the choir of boys preparing for High Holiday Services in 1931. Being part of the choir, even as a child, was ironic. Dad could barely carry a tune.

Hebrew School Choir.
Dad seated in Row 1, far left

Technology, even a hundred years ago, was advancing at a rapid speed. Dad built the family's first radio, a crystal set, in electric shop at Memorial Junior High in the early 1930's. He had no money for the headphones for his radio so he devised a way to generate the needed funds. His Friday lunch allowance was twenty-five cents. But his friend used to steal hot dogs and sell them two for five cents which left Dad saving twenty cents each week towards his headphones.

He eventually saved enough to buy the earphones and particularly relished listening to "Amos and Andy," one of the first radio comedy shows on air. The episodes centered around two black comedians with get-rich quick schemes. The sitcom, first broadcast in 1928, was set in Harlem, New York. Dad got in the habit of wearing his earphones every night at dinner to listen to the antics of the characters. Somewhat curious, one day his father questioned "I don't know vat could be so important that you are listening to. So vat is it?" "Pa, you wanna listen?" Dad offered. Dad never got possession of the earphones at dinner from that day on. Louis had the earpieces placed over his ears before the family sat down. He was always amazed, wondering "Vere's the electricity?" Finally, when Dad was about fourteen, Louis bought a Philco radio and the entire family gathered around to listen to Amos and Andy. The show was a popular hit on the air until 1960.

At San Diego High School, Dad's friends were a melting pot of color, class, and ethnicity. A good friend, Amos Manuel, was a young Black teen working several jobs to contribute to his family's financial stability. Amos and his brother carried a box around town shining shoes on the weekends. They built up a reputation and continued for decades servicing customers from a stand with a sign advertising *Amos' Shoeshine*. The stand was located on 8th Avenue near C Street in the heart of downtown. Neither Amos nor Dad ever forgot his roots.

Whenever Dad drove downtown to the popular deli, Bohemian Bakery, he had the window rolled down expecting to see his old friend. The wind blew his comb over so long strands of hair stood straight up. When Dad rounded the corner and the shoeshine stand came into view, he couldn't contain his enthusiasm. "Hello-o-o-o Amos Manuel" he shouted in a voice that expressed total delight. His entire arm hung out the window and he waved his arm frantically as his eyes diverted from the road. He had an ear to ear grin when Amos glanced his way. Then a voice bellowed through the air as Amos looked up from the wingtip he was polishing, rag in hand, "Hell-o-o-o-o Solly Schultz." Their friendship saw no boundaries.

A sports enthusiast, Dad participated in minor sport activities in high school including basketball, Junior Varsity football and Interclass track. He was a fairly good athlete but his spirit superseded his ability. He would be the first to admit he did not excel at any of these sports. He finally discovered wrestling and found it a good fit and success at the high school level until he broke his leg in an unfortunate match.

Wrestling was a good "match"
for Dad

5

So Vat Chu Gonna Do?

Dad was embarrassed. From elementary school to high school he never invited friends to his house. He was ashamed that the place he called home only had an outdoor toilet. He chose to meet with his many friends at the playground, at the library, at their house, anyplace but at his house.

"Will you look at that?" Dad marveled. After graduating from San Diego High School, Louis, Anna, and Dad moved from the boarding house to a home with a shake roof on Granada Street in North Park. This area of the city had a substantial Jewish community that supported a kosher butcher. But what was most notable was inside the house with the dark brown wood siding. The home had an indoor toilet.

For his parents, the end of Dad's high school years were expected to be the end of his formal education. "So son, vat chu gonna do when school is over? You need to getta job." Higher education seemed like an unnecessary indulgence. "So vat is more school gonna do for you?" Louis asked, referring to Dad's three siblings who had not finished high school. "You need to earn a living like your brother and sisters. Why Lil is a big shot bookkeeper and Jack makes money fixing machines....So?"

But Dad had a goal, and even though he had no support from his parents, he was determined to go to college. He had no passion for any specific field, just ambition and drive to be successful. He had no idea what opportunities were available.

He was accepted at San Diego State College that had a student enrollment of around 2,000 in 1937. College life was uncharted territory for his family. He knew that he would have a place to live and understood that was where the financial support ended. Dad needed a job, or many, to pay for tuition and books.

He entered his freshman year and found college a whole new kind of education. With naiveté, he pledged a local fraternity that in later years affiliated with the national fraternity Pi Kappa Alpha. Dad's grit and outgoing personality fit in and the brotherhood opened his eyes to a world of parties, alcohol, and girls. He avoided drinking after observing his father's steady use of alcohol while growing up. Plus he exhibited a shyness around girls. It was possibly because no girl he met at the fraternity parties interested him.

In his senior year he decided that participating in the fraternity brotherhood was just too expensive. He was making ends meet, but only by working in the school cafe during lunch and working as an usher at the coliseum at 15th and E three nights a week. On Saturday and Sunday he either worked in the produce department for Safeway or at any other store with a produce department that would give him the work.

Dad's other part time jobs through college included furniture sales, working at a tuna cannery, working at the 1935 World Exposition in Balboa Park and at the Del Mar Race Track. He learned on-the-job, hated menial assembly work, had a knack for merchandising and sales, and an innate understanding of business. Dad possessed a strong work ethic and chutzpah.

Working at the Del Mar racetrack, he caught a glimpse of privilege; the life of the rich and famous. The racetrack, located right off the beach, was built by the Thoroughbred Club in 1937 with founding members being popular crooner, Bing Crosby, and Hollywood Irish actor, Pat O'Brien. When the Del Mar Racetrack opened, Bing Crosby was at the gate to greet the fans. With Bing Crosby and Pat O'Brien came all the celebrity glitter of Hollywood. During the racetrack's early years — 1937 to 1941 — stars arrived in abundance. The stars came out to be seen, the most famous ranging from Dorothy Lamour to W.C. Fields to Edgar Bergen to Ava Gardner.

Barbecues and softball games on the beach at Del Mar during racing season included celebrities as well as low wage employees. One day Pat O'Brien approached Dad. "Hey kid, how about putting together a softball team? The jockeys need something to do in their free time and they can play against the employees. Do that. Will ya?"

Being a sports fan, this was right up Dad's alley. He formed a team comprised of ticket sellers, ushers, and other minimum wage workers, to challenge the jockeys. Many of these were school teachers working summer jobs and athletic skills were not their strength. On the contrary, the jockeys were great athletes and were very competitive. Dad, in the spirit of competition, recruited some San Diego friends who played in the city's Triple A fast pitch softball leagues. These included the top pitchers who were passed off as track maintenance workers. The fake track workers consistently beat the jockeys. The rivals took the games seriously, but the jockeys balked when the true identity of their opponents was discovered. "That ain't fair," they complained.

A high point of his employment at the racetrack was the incredible story of the "amazing race" between two thoroughbreds on August 12, 1938, that was well documented in history books. The race came about due to a friendship between Bing Crosby and Lin Howard, the son of the owner of the thoroughbred Seabiscuit, Charles Howard. Lin Howard and Bing Crosby together founded Binglin Stables, with the goal of raising winning horses. Competing with his father, Lin was determined to run his Argentinean bred horse Ligaroti against champion Seabiscuit. The publicity surrounding the race between the two champion purebreds was astounding and made the Del Mar Racetrack known far and wide. There was a record crowd when Seabiscuit beat Ligaroti by a nose in an exciting battle. Dad shared the thrilling day over and over and kept a glossy black and white photo of the winning horse as he crossed the finish line.

Professional boxing was sanctioned in 1921 and boxing events became popular. Fight clubs flourished throughout the country. The 3,512 seat Coliseum Federal Athletic Club was located in downtown San Diego and became a major boxing venue in southern California. Dad worked part-time as an usher at the Coliseum, providing him the opportunity to witness championship matches, including fights involving the light heavyweight champion, Archie Moore.

On one occasion, after a particularly brutal fight, Archie Moore, battered and bleeding, needed a transfusion. When volunteers were called for, Dad offered.

"Hey, my blood type is AB. My blood plasma can be universally used so I am ready to donate to the champ."

Years later when meeting Archie Moore at a charity event, Dad approached Moore.

"Hey Archie, I bet you remember that fight at the Coliseum when you needed some blood? Well, I was right there to give you some of mine."

Moore responded "Oh yeah. I can't forget that fight."

He pulled out a photo, and signed it "To my blood brother, Archie Moore."

Success in high school prompted Dad to join the college wrestling team after his leg healed from the break he had sustained the previous year. He also joined the track team and threw the javelin far enough to earn a freshman sweater.

During his sophomore year the college newspaper, The Aztec, ran an ad: "WANTED: Spirited and full of energy - four sophomores, two juniors, and one senior. Needed to manage the Aztec football team. Must be able and dependable to attend all games." "Hmmmm, sounds like a good time," Dad reasoned, then sent in his application. After two weeks he was notified that he was chosen as the Senior Manager. "Wow, they want me to be the

H$_2$O Schultz,
Football Team Manager

Senior Manager. My application must have been impressive." This was a point of pride until he discovered that no senior had applied. His enthusiasm was not dampened and he served for three years as Senior Manager.

Dad was so dedicated to the spirit of the football team that the story of H$_2$O Schultz lived on long after he served as manager.

"We had a huge water cart for football games at home that we also took on road trips. It had a tank that held 50 gallons of water and had six faucets on top for the players to drink from. I used to recruit someone to help push it and they got in free to see the game. The hand pump was instrumental in getting up the pressure so the water would flow. I wore a sweatshirt with 'H$_2$0' on the back and it became a symbol and I was nicknamed 'H$_2$0' Schultz. It was known throughout the campus that I would wear the sweater to every single game until we lost."

The worn and holey sweatshirt had faded from the original bright red of the school colors by the end of his managing duties. But the treasured garment held a place of honor in Dad's drawer for decades as one of many prized possessions.

When football season ended in his sophomore year, Dad was approached to manage the baseball team. A dedicated Aztec, he agreed. "Sure, I'll do it." He was rewarded with a lifetime pass to all the San Diego State College games. After years of use, the pass was as worn as his H_2O sweater.

Dad combined his knowledge of wrestling with entertainment and found a fun and rewarding outlet. Performing "Professional Wrestling Matches" was Dad's forte. These matches were much in demand at guys-only fraternity parties known as smokers, Dad's Day, and other social functions around campus. Dad put on the show with his closest friend from High School, Eddie Priceler. Disguised as the "Masked Marvel," Dad was always the bad guy and Eddie was always the good guy. Newspaper articles enthusiastically promoted the events.

"Sol Schultz, the mild mannered lad who ushers at the Coliseum and sports a letterman's sweater won last year as manager of San Diego State's football team, steps into the role of wrestler at the college gym tonight when he meets a masked opponent dubbed "The Slashing Shadow", in a one-fall match that is the feature attraction at the men's stag held at mid-semester each year for incoming students." Even without disclosing this in the news, no one was fooled. Everyone knew Sol Schultz, even in his mask.

Between managing the Aztecs sports teams, participating in fraternity activities and working multiple part-time jobs,

Dad squeezed in class time, though he favored other aspects of college life.

Giving politics a shot in his senior year, he decided to run for class office. He was elected vice president of the class of 1941. He never ran for office again though he treasured his gavel and passed it on to his granddaughter, Lindsay, when she was elected ASB President of her high school.

6

There Are No Small Parts

In 1938 the "Masked Marvel" was called into the office of Deborah Smith, head of the Music Department.

"Sol, we are honored to have a very famous performance of a ballet on Saturday," she explained excitedly. "The Ballets Russes de Monte Carlo will be here in San Diego with a performance at the Russ Auditorium at San Diego High School. It is the largest and best auditorium in the city. This will be quite the event. And guess what?"

Dad couldn't guess. He wasn't in Ms Smith's class, he definitely couldn't dance, and he sang off-key. He had no idea, until she interrupted the varied questions circulating through his brain.

"The director, Sol Hurok, wants a few students to appear in the ballet. I thought of you. You would be glorious. You have done an excellent job as stage manager of the Music Department. You showed how capable you were when the "Student Prince" was performed in the Wegeforth Bowl in Balboa Park."

"I would love to, but you know me, Ms. Smith. I can't sing, let alone dance in a ballet," Dad chuckled.

"No, no," she replied, "I am sure it is just a walk on, with no singing and, thank the Lord, no ballet for you or the other three boys that are going to be in it. And remember," she continued, "you will be on stage with the greatest ballerina of our time — Alicia Markova."

Dad had a few questions for Ms. Smith before he would agree to accept the challenge.

Q: "Do I have to learn lines?"

A: "I don't know"

Q: "Must I wear anything special"

A: "I don't know"

Q: "How much will I be paid?"

A: "I don't know if you will be paid."

Dad was satisfied with her answers. As he left her office she added a few encouraging words "It's probably just a walk-on part." Walk Dad could do….and he would do it with actual professionals.

The total of four students were given orders to "report at noon and don't be late." They were so nervous that they reported at eleven then were told to come back at noon. The boys walked a block and a half away to the Silver Castle System and gorged on five cent cheeseburgers and five cent colas.

They reported back at the requested time. The assistant director took over and handed them some raggedy clothes to change into. He then took them to a sedan chair and the four of them had to practice carrying the lead stand-in and setting the chair down without dumping the stand-in.

In another scene they were supposed to enact a four piece orchestra. The instruments were fake and Dad was the violinist with a bow and no strings. He was supposed to saw away like he was playing but the bow kept getting caught on the bridge and he had to pull up to release it so he could "saw" again.

The boys "performed" two shows that day. When they had changed after the second show Mr. Hurok lined the State College students up. "You work afternoon show, yes?" and handed each boy a dollar. "You work night show, yes?" and handed each another dollar. Then he shook hands with each boy and said he was Sol Hurok and asked each boy his name. He had a big grin when Dad answered "Sol Schultz, Mr. Hurok."

He invited the boys to come to Los Angeles to work four shows. The offer was easily passed up by every student.

On Monday there was a note on the official bulletin board from Dr. Ray Perry for Dad to come to his office.

"Sol," he said, "I hate ballet, but being a good son I accompanied my mother Saturday night to see the Ballet Russes de Monte Carlo, and for the first time I really enjoyed it, especially your violin playing. I first noticed the bow seemed to be caught on the bridge. I reached over and borrowed my mother's opera glasses and lo and behold — Sol Schultz, famous water boy for the football team among other things, on the stage with the great Alicia Markova and playing a violin like no one before!"

He continued, "When I told my mother who you were, she said it was impossible as such a great talent would have only professionals, not college students."

She was right. For two dollars, Dad was a professional.

7

Getting to Know You

It was in Skull and Dagger, a college theater group, that Dad noticed a cute freshman named Charlotte. He had befriended a student actress named Ethel Fried. Ethel was a tall redhead, born with drama as part of her DNA. She was a capable performer and she could create a memorable episode around watching a flower bloom. He liked Ethel, particularly when he found out that Charlotte was Ethel's younger sister.

Charlotte, my mom, though tiny in stature, possessed a broad easy smile and ready laugh. She was bouncy, energetic, sweet, and well-liked. She participated in theater though she did not possess the passion to be center stage. Dad loved the theater, though his shyness overtook his acting ability with regards to asking Charlotte out on a date.

Mom flourished in college, balancing classes with many clubs, both academic and social. Dad's time was parceled out between work, fraternity, and with what little time was left, academics. He was eager to get to know Charlotte Joy Fried.

A perfect opportunity soon presented itself with the help of Dad's "Pa." "Wow, I can't believe it. This beats all. Thanks a ton, Pa," Dad grinned broadly. He was commuting to San Diego State College in 1937, his sophomore year, when his father surprised him with a much needed and most appreciated gift. He was ecstatic to be the recipient of a '32 Chevy with two fender wells and a rumble seat. "Sol, de car cost me lotsa money. I paid $350 cash for it. You gonna have to pay for de gas, some where to keep it, insurance, and fix it if anything goes wrong......and be careful driving it. People drive meshuga (crazy) here." Dad's heart beat rapidly and his chest puffed out with excitement as he gazed with pride at the used vehicle. *I'm a real college guy now. I have my own car.*

He didn't mind that most of the money from his part-time work was needed to pay for college expenses and now he was responsible for upkeep on his car. He had spent the past months hitching rides to college and struggled to secure transportation to his multiple jobs located throughout the city. Now that he had wheels, he could manage his schedule easier. Thus, his self-confidence grew. He was ready to take a leap of faith. He had his eyes on a special girl.

San Diego's weather is notably the most consistent in the country; fluctuating between cold, forty degrees, and hot, eighty-five degrees. The weather forecast for frost warnings are minimal throughout the year. Sunstroke warnings in the sunny city are more common. The lack of real seasonal changes generate unmatched excitement when the Laguna Mountains, a one hour drive east from San Diego, get an occasional flurry of snow. Often it is just a few inches that settle on the ground when the twigs and leaves are still visible through the thin blanket of white. But to San Diegans this means an exodus by anyone who has the time and means to get to the mountains. Mittens and knit caps are retrieved from the bottom of drawers as hordes of people make their way to the snow.

On one of those rare winter days in 1938 a storm pushed through the mountains. Dad was asked to join a couple of friends, including Ethel Fried, in an escapade of snow play the following weekend. He found himself literally in the driver's seat for he was the only one who actually owned a car. He agreed to chauffeur the group on one condition. "Sure, I'll go. As long as Charlotte Fried comes with us and sits in the front with me, I'll drive."

He envisioned the trip would be the perfect way to get the much pined for date with Mom. He thought she was cute, had a fun personality, and he was aware that she was Jewish. He had tried to catch her attention in class by placing himself in her presence while joking with the other thespians. But until this point he hadn't gotten up the nerve to approach her directly and ask for a date. The weekend rendezvous was his chance.

He casually approached her one day at Skull and Dagger. "Hey Charlotte, I hear there's snow in the mountains. Whadaya think about going there with me and a couple others on Sunday?" "H-m-m-m," she hesitated, not sure whether Dad was asking for an actual date or not. After a few seconds she decided that a snow outing was worth whatever his reason was. She had spent the first years of her life in snowy Idaho and was eager to see California snow. "Sure, I'd love to go to the snow. It sounds like fun."

Charlotte rode in the passenger's seat and Charlotte's sister, Ethel, and one other friend, piled into the rumble seat. The rumble seat, an upholstered exterior seat, folded into the deck of an automobile and was popular in pre-World War II cars.

The conversation flowed easily. Mom was loquacious so there was rarely a moment of silence. Finally Dad got a few hours of quality time with the girl he had had his eye on for weeks. The group spent hours having snowball fights, building snowmen, and sliding down hillsides. By the end of the day the party of four was wet, cold, and tired.

The day had been memorable, especially for the two sharing the front seat. Their snow day was the beginning of a flirty friendship. It was yet to be seen whether the initial attraction was enough for two young people with different personalities from different backgrounds to lead to a lasting relationship and love.

1938: Mom & Dad's first date in the Laguna Mountains

8

Charlotte Joy

Just who was Charlotte Joy Fried; the girl who intrigued the "Masked Marvel?"

Her mother, Lottie Oliner, who we called Nanny, was born February 20, 1888, in Leadville, Colorado. Mom's maternal grandparents had immigrated from Eastern Europe following the silver rush of opportunity to the mining town of Leadville, Colorado. The family was affiliated with Temple Israel, a synagogue built for $4,000 and dedicated in 1884. There were four Oliner children: Jake, Fannie, Lottie, and Mike.

When Lottie was a young child the family followed the silver to Park City, Utah, a town with a population at the time of 2,850. The family settled in the middle of town at the top of a long flight of stairs leading to a row of houses above the street still in existence today.

In the early 1900s Park City was picturesque with copper mining buckets at intervals hanging overhead throughout the city. There were no other Jewish families in Park City when the Oliners came to town and the only church was a Methodist church. Since all the neighborhood children went to the Methodist Church, Lottie and her closest friend Ida, who was Catholic, wanted to go also.

Children went to the pulpit and were confirmed as members of the Methodist Church when they reached thirteen years of age. One Sunday Lottie and Ida arrived at the church and discovered that this was the day of Confirmation. She stood up and whispered to her best friend, "I don't think my mother will like this." Her friend agreed. "If you're not doing it, I'm not either." They both ran out of the church and never looked back. Utah was overwhelmingly a Mormon state, though there were no Mormons in Park City. "The Only Gentile Town in Utah" was printed on the masthead of the newspaper.

Lottie got her first real job in Park City as a telephone operator. In the 1890s women telephone operators often spoke to the same small group of customers every day. This created an intimacy between the operator and caller as they both grew to recognize who was on the line connecting the calls. Operators could be counted on to have all sorts of information at hand, such as the names and addresses of local customers, the latest news, weather, and sports results, the correct time of day, and, of course, an inside track on Park City gossip.

One day Lottie was at work diligently doing her job at the switchboard. She picked up the incoming call and in her most sophisticated voice she said, "Hello, this is Lottie, may I help you?" "Yes, connect me to the Purple Parlor" responded a male in a cocky voice filled with unseen swagger.

The Purple Parlor was part of a row of sixteen houses of ill repute. It was the well known and respected brothel serving the miners in Park City who came to socialize, drink, gamble, and partake in the activities of a popular house of prostitution.

Lottie was astounded as she recognized the familiar voice of her brother. She lost her professional composure and blurted out in a voice two octaves higher than she had spoken previously "JAKEY, is that you?" The line quickly went dead.

Mom's father, Morris Fried, my grandfather we called Morris Daddy, was born on June 15, 1882, in the small town of Skaudville, Taurage, outside of Vilnius, Lithuania. He was a bright young man with a fair complexion, blue eyes, a thin wiry build and at full height was 5' 5". Morris was one of many siblings but was a small sickly child with tuberculosis. Hoping to improve his health, Morris was sent from his village in Lithuania to America to live with his first cousin, Mordecai Kaplan.

Mordecai Kaplan would become legendary. He was known as the father of Reconstruction Judaism. He modernized the traditions of Judaism and initiated Bat Mitzvah's for girls. Cousin Mordecai was ahead of his time. He preached equality for girls long before it was in vogue, most likely because he fathered four daughters.

Lottie and Morris met in Salt Lake City, Utah and were married on April 16, 1916. In a physical, social, and academic sense, these two were diametrically opposite. As slight as Morris was, Lottie was short but full figured with wavy hair and dark penetrating brown eyes, one of which occasionally wandered. Morris' coke-bottle glasses over his light eyes corrected his near-sightedness and were an immediate focus of his sharp facial features. His physical appearance alone portrayed Morris as serious and intellectual. By the same token, Lottie appeared approachable, warm, and cuddly. Morris favored discussing political issues while Lottie favored charity socials. But both believed in helping the underdog and contributing financially to better the world.

Morris was proud of his adopted country, becoming a naturalized U.S. citizen on January 18, 1915, at the age of 32. He took his civic duty sincerely. He was happy to pay taxes, telling friends who complained about them "Don't complain. Be thankful you are the one who is making enough money to pay the taxes."

Various members of Morris' family migrated to the small towns in Idaho and opened

Fried Family:
Ethel, Miriam, Lottie, Charlotte, Morris

general stores. Morris and Lottie also spread their wings, moving to Ashton, Idaho, the last town before Yellowstone where they opened a mercantile store. Two daughters, Ethel and Miriam, were born in this small town and within a couple of years, a third daughter, my mom Charlotte, arrived on May 3, 1920. Again the Fried family found themselves to be the only Jewish family in the community. When her friends wanted companions, Mom and her sisters attended the local Methodist Church.

On occasion Lottie traveled by train two hundred and fifty miles back to Salt Lake City to visit her family. During one trip she purchased a very expensive handbag that she had admired on a previous journey. Upon arriving back in Ashton, she walked in the house, took off her coat and placed her prized possession on the sofa.

Mom ran into the room, excited to see her mother. With a leap, she jumped on the sofa shrieking in her child's high-pitched voice "Mama, I missed you so much. I'm so glad you're home." At that moment there was a sharp *cr-cr-crack* emanating from the sofa. Little Charlotte had landed on the

Mom in Ashton, Idaho

purse, crushing it. Lottie gasped, then all sound and movement came to a halt. In slow motion Lottie inched towards the sofa, fearful what she would witness. Her forehead furrowed and her eyes widened. For a brief minute she stood stunned. The mirror inside her handbag was broken beyond repair. Instantly she gathered her thoughts, her frown softened, and her eyes narrowed. The corners of her mouth turned upward and she smiled, opened her arms, and grabbed Mom for a hug. "It doesn't matter," Lottie said. "If money can replace it, we are not going to worry about it. I am just glad to be home with my girls."

While there was no Jewish community in Ashton, the Fried family would gather in Pocatello, Idaho, with relatives for Passover in the spring and in the fall for the High Holy Days, Rosh Hashanah and Yom Kippur. There was no synagogue nearby, so the men would put on their own religious services for the family.

Though they had no organized religious services, the ethnic and cultural connection to Judaism for the Fried family was deep. Historical records of B'nai B'rith of Southern Idaho show that in 1923 M. Fried was one of 36 founding members of this philanthropic and humanitarian organization with the mission of enhancing Jewish identity through strengthening of Jewish family life. This was significant since the area was populated with only 120 Jewish people including women and children.

When the girls got older Morris realized that all of the older cousins went off to college and never came back to Idaho. He wanted to find a home where his children would want to return to after college. He felt it was time to leave Ashton and Idaho altogether. During the winter of 1932 Morris visited a friend from Idaho who had moved to San Diego. He owned the local newspaper in the beach community of Ocean Beach.

During that visit, Morris called home to his wife, Lottie, bursting with enthusiasm. "I've found heaven on earth and we are moving to San Diego." He kept his word, selling the store, packing their worldly goods and leaving with Lottie and their three daughters for California. They fell in love with Point Loma, the peninsula community located a few miles from downtown.

Sister Ethel was tall and slim, with a toothy smile and self-assured confidence. Sister Miriam was a brunette of medium height and a quiet manner. Mom, Charlotte Joy, a spirited brunette, was twelve years old when the family moved south to California. She inherited qualities from both her mother and father. She took after her father in size and intellect, but her empathy, kindness, and positive outlook, were inherited from her mother.

The Fried family bought a white Spanish style pre-war home built in 1928 and settled in. They were the only Jewish family in Ashton and in Point Loma they were one of three Jewish families. They joined Temple Beth Israel, a reform congregation of sixty families that had been relocated from Heritage Park in the Old Town area of San Diego to 3rd and Laurel in 1926. The three sisters were confirmed in the Jewish faith at Temple Beth Israel as each completed the tenth grade. Though Morris did not follow many Jewish customs, he strongly believed in supporting a synagogue. "It doesn't matter if you want to go to the temple and participate in services or not. It is our responsibility to support it for those who want to go and can't afford it."

The business experience Lottie and Morris brought with them to California was acquired from the store they had owned in Ashton, Idaho. So it seemed natural for Morris and Lottie to open up a store in San Diego. Fried's Woman's Clothing and Shoes was located in Ocean Beach, literally three blocks from the Pacific Ocean. Flower arrangements from well-wishers lined the shelves during the grand opening.

The store was a success and Lottie and Morris became pillars of the community. They generously gave free clothing and shoes to women in need and to needy children at Ocean Beach Elementary School. Morris was content that he got his daily exercise by walking the three miles from home to the store.

The Fried girls spent their free time working in the store where Mom remembered the grab bag promotion. A popular grab bag gimmick was being held for the customers. For a few cents a shopper could take a chance by choosing a grab bag. A few of the bags included a crisp one dollar bill along with an accessory or novelty. Without anyone's knowledge Mom watched the bags being filled in the storeroom and where a dollar had been placed. She approached her father, "Daddy, I want to take a chance and buy a grab bag. I have my allowance to pay for it." "Okay Charlotte," Morris replied. "You might not get a dollar but if you want to spend your money that way, go ahead." Mom's surprised expression did not give away the ruse after she chose a bag with the prize dollar. Her guilt, told to us decades later, remained long after the dollar was spent.

Both Lottie and Morris became involved in a number of diverse organizations. Lottie joined the non-denominational Eastern Stars and Morris joined the Masons, where members must acknowledge a Supreme Being.

Lottie was a founder of the San Diego Hebrew Home for the Aged, became a life member of Hadassah and Brandeis, and worked for the National Council of Jewish Federations and Welfare Funds developed in 1932. But with no formal Jewish education, and childhood attendance at the Methodist

Church, the only song Lottie could remember the words to throughout her life was "Onward Christian Soldiers."

Point Loma High School included grades 7-12, with a total Jewish population of six students. Three of those students were the Fried girls, two students were from Ocean Beach, and one from Mission Beach. Mom's high school days at Point Loma were full of activities: Girl Reserves, Glee Club, Drama, Spanish Club, and the Pep Club.

She participated in gymnastics until she broke her leg. This did not discourage her in her mid eighties from demonstrating her ability to stand on her head when the family went on a picnic or when a grandchild requested it. When Mom was a senior, the Point Loma yearbook of 1937 listed the following:

Mom. Point Loma High School Graduation June 1937

'Charlotte Fried, Nickname: Charlie, Pet expression: M'love, Ambition: Talk about Miss Clark when....(this must have been an inside joke), Fate: Giant in circus.'

She was an excellent student whose parents valued education. There was no question that the three Fried girls would attend college. It was not a choice.

Lottie's family in Salt Lake City needed financial support so Morris and Lottie sent money to Utah. Thus, Mom had no options to attend college out of the area. She was accepted to San Diego State College in 1937 which proved to be a decision of fate.

The history of San Diego State University on the University's website shows that by 1921 the Normal School founded in 1897 with limited offerings to train prospective teachers became known as San Diego State Teachers College, a four year public institution. In 1935 educational offerings were increased beyond teacher education and the name changed to San Diego State College. Though the name changed, Mom wanted to be a teacher and pursued her degree in education.

Right from the beginning of her freshman year at San Diego State College she became active in a variety of social and academic clubs. She was accepted to Kappa Delta Pi, an honor society in education. Her positive outlook was evident in a term paper for English 134 titled "Is Happiness a Bubble?" She received an A on the six page paper and ended it by concluding "The important thing then is not what comes to you but what you bring to yourself. The individual makes his own happiness..."

She was chosen for Cetza, a freshman women's service organization and she was elected president in her junior year.

"Little Girl" at San Diego State College

In an article in the Aztec newspaper, Mom was introduced: "Charlotte Fried, President of Cetza... Junior... Theater Guild, Skull & Dagger (Secretary)... getting elementary teaching credentials... one of three sisters... a gold football hangs around her neck (but she also likes other sports)...makes her own clothes... loves malted milks...hates dressing in her sandwiches...perennially losing her hair ribbon...presided charmingly at Cetza alumnae banquet Wednesday... has taken aerobic dancing since a small child...with her five feet in height is "little girl" of the campus."

During her senior year, Mom was tapped for Cap and Gown, a national honorary senior woman's organization, whose members are chosen for 'scholarship, leadership, and service.

The "little girl" of the campus had made a name for herself. She had fully entrenched herself in college and she had a boyfriend. Now the question was whether the gold football hanging around her neck would lead to a 'touchdown and a win.'

9

"Bei Mir Bis Du"

The journey to the Laguna Mountains boosted Dad's confidence. He had played a winning hand and now he was encouraged and eager for a follow up. Being a true romantic, Dad asked Mom on their first "real" date on Valentine's Day, February 14, 1938. The next day Dad sent Mom a Western Union telegram that expressed how he felt. *"Roses are Red, Violets are Blue, Sugar is Sweet, Bei Mir Bist Du Shein"* *(To Me You're Beautiful.)* The line was borrowed from the most popular Yiddish song of the day sung by the Andrew Sisters. Romance was in full bloom indicated by this first of many poems, love notes, and sentimental verses Dad continued to send.

Mom's and Dad's backgrounds were vastly different. Mom's middle class family had some social standing in San Diego's Jewish community. Though Dad's family joined the synagogue, his parents kept to themselves. Higher formal education was valued and expected by Mom's parents while Dad's family was convinced that hard work rather than education was necessary to make a living and succeed.

Dad's college experience opened his eyes to possibilities beyond the surroundings of his childhood. For three years, in between college classes and many jobs, Dad found time to spend with Mom. He arrived at Mom's Point Loma home directly from his job at the tuna cannery with the smell of fish permeating the air around him. His clothes reeked of cigarette smoke after a night of ushering at the Coliseum. But Mom didn't mind a bit.

In June, 1939, Mom and her friends from the Jay Dee college club rented a house in Laguna Beach, an hour and a half drive north of San Diego. The coeds looked forward to a week of relaxation and beach fun shared with girlfriends. Mom casually invited Dad to come visit during the week.

After calculating the expenses associated with his car and school he came to the realization that he couldn't afford the visit. He rationalized *I'll have to miss work and pay for gas both ways on top of it. It just cost too much.* But his desire to be with Mom overruled his logical thinking. He decided to work through most of the break, volunteering for extra shifts to earn enough for the trip. In the end, he was more than eager to make the drive. He figured his girl was worth the five gallons of gas that cost $.19 per gallon and equaled a third of his daily wage.

Dad's manner of courting Mom proved that he was different than her past boyfriends. His sense of humor and creativity were often expressed in the written word. He was a true romantic.

This poem was sent as a 'thank you' for a lunch prepared by the girl he was enamored with:

Charlotte Dear,
Here are the dishes
From a lunch so delishus
Made by a sweet little girl.

Everything was just dandy
From hot soup to candy
You're a gem, sweetheart- a pearl.
Love, Sol

A note asking for a date was passed to Mom during class. How could she resist?

June twenty 5,
Dear Charlotte,

I'm sending you my pitcher and a note. Wood yew like to go to a showhouse Sunday nite? I will call you up Sat nite on the telephone and I hope you can go.

Affeckshunally, Sol

Mom had taken dance lessons for years as a child. Even as an adult, she still loved to dance. It had never crossed Dad's mind that this was a necessary skill. Desiring not to embarrass himself, and to impress this somewhat sophisticated miss, he took ballroom classes at Arthur Murray Dance Studio. He wanted to surprise Mom by inviting her to go dancing with him so he did his best to learn the steps. His conclusion at the end of the lessons was that he danced the way he played bridge- "not so hot."

Exactly two years after their first date, the sentiment in a 1940 homemade Valentine's Card made one thing clear:

I know I'm no Adonis
With curly locks of gold-

I'm not the strongest Hercules
So tall and strong and bold.
I'm not a star in movies,
Like Tracy or Gable or Taylor-
I'm not a champion athlete,
From "Cal" or State or Baylor.
I haven't got a special car,
With radio, or wheels of white-
Everything doesn't always work,
(Remember—you pound the light!)
Yet I've got more than anyone
On this ever so wide earth-
I've got my little "Punkie"
Who's more than anything's worth.
I can't write very good poems,
(You've seen samples of quite a few)
The only one I want to write is-
I Love You,
Your Solly

Their relationship had normal ups and downs but it appears that Dad's gift of humor and Mom's forgiving heart got them through the low points. Their worn and tattered scrapbook from their college and courting years never disclosed what their first argument was about. But in her quiet way "Punkie" must have encouraged a letter of apology. Dad sent an endearing message that pleased her enough to save it.

Reports from Dan'l Cupid, Jr., scorekeeper for the Happy Hearts Baseball Team show that the last nites error was an unintentional one. Please change this in your book and it will never happen again. In other words - forgive me, Sol.

Mom, an easy-going good sport, was usually up for any kind of adventure and enjoyed surprises. Dad was sure she would get into the spirit of the Farmer's Frolic, a popular fraternity party. In keeping with the theme, the entrance to the barn party involved going down a slide. Contrary to her usual good nature, Mom was adamant. "I'm not going down the slide. I just don't want to," she insisted. She wouldn't budge and no coaxing could convince her otherwise. The fraternity gatekeepers finally opened the barn door to let her in avoiding the slide altogether. It was years before Dad found out the reason for her hesitancy. Mom always had a habit when dressing of putting on her underpants last. When Dad arrived to pick her up she wasn't quite ready. In a hurry, she merely forgot to put her underpants on.

The college years passed by quickly. The fraternity parties, clubs, athletic events, classes and other aspects of student life were coming to an end.

Even while working his part-time job at the Del Mar Racetrack, Dad's thoughts were of Mom. In August 1941 he sent her a colorful postcard of the "Mission Walls and Cool Arches" at the Del Mar Turf Club. On it he wrote *"Dear Charl; From a lovely track to a beautiful girl. Don't forget, ever- pretty soon. Sol"* It was two months before they were to be married.

Mom and Dad had found they were soulmates. The relationship between the girl who occasionally forgot her underpants and the scrappy boy who occasionally smelled like fish or cigarettes had stood the test of time.

10

Creative

Dad's distinctive writing style got kudos when his fictional story "The Dummy" was published in the fall 1937 San Diego State College literary magazine, El Palenque. His stories were unique, his characters alive, and his endings always had an unexpected twist.

Leslie Shoemaker, Dad's friend, was Sports Editor of the San Diego Sun newspaper. He liked "The Dummy," incorporating it in his column. "You've heard about Sol "Solly" Schultz, the genial State College football manager who did more to keep the Aztecs alive this past season than any other one individual on the campus. Solly, however, is not just an ordinary manager. He's ambidextrous with his gray cells. He's also a writer….with a football fiction as interesting as it is novel."

Dad became a prolific contributor to the literary magazine. In the fall of 1939, he wrote a short story called "The Farm" that was published in the magazine. In the Spring, "The Warning" made the El Palenque.

The Daily Aztec, the college newspaper, featured Dad's popular column on sports. The paper included his football selections for the week. He was always clever, funny, and often self-deprecating. He had no qualms about apologizing for his weekly choices.

"I am so sorry I could not pick 'em for you last week but if you remember correctly, I did not do so well two weeks ago. In fact to tell the truth I indulged, well, I imbibed, oh hell, I went to the barbershop and the fellow made seven straight passes....I mean I bet on the teams I picked and when the smoke settled I had not the price of a ....Well, I could not get my typewriter out of hock. So there!"

Dad was able to combine his writing skills with his love of drama as a member of Skull & Dagger, the San Diego State College Dramatic Society and the oldest student organization on campus. There was a need to raise funds for Skull and Dagger in 1939 so Dad rose to the challenge. After many months he had written the script for a musicomedy called "Fit to Print." He was ready to produce it but now he needed music—for which he had no talent.

The great musician, Joe Liggins, was a black pianist and vocalist who had moved to San Diego in 1932. His band, Joe Liggins and his Honeydrippers, was often included on the Billboard magazine charts, topping the charts in 1945 with a song called "The Honeydripper." Joe Liggins was not in college at the time, but some of the students knew Joe from high school. Dad was hopeful that Joe might help him complete the script with original music. He persuaded a friend to give him Joe's address.

One night he got up his nerve and drove to Joe's house. It It was a bold move, and he wasn't sure whether or not he would be thrown out on the street. He gingerly knocked on the door. When the door opened, the dominant sounds of gospel music accompanied by hand clapping filled the night air. When he was escorted in, he realized Joe's mother was conducting church services to some twenty people and singing hymns with Joe on the piano. He sat respectfully "as quiet as a church mouse" as he heard the soulful strain '...There will be peace in the valley for me, some day.' His thoughts were far from his mission as the synchronized voices drifted through the walls joined by the accomplished pianist.

Following the service Joe and Dad retreated to his '32 Chevy, complete with rumble seat, fender wells, and two spare tires installed in the front fenders. With flashlight in hand, Dad read parts of the script where he thought songs should be inserted. Joe wrote six songs and members of the cast wrote the lyrics to match circumstances and situations in the play.

Opening night was a sellout plus one. At that time, San Diego State College was in the back country of San Diego and small wildlife was in abundance. The diverse animal population in the area included: possums, rattlesnakes, squirrels, coyotes, and the ever present skunk. The one who made a grand entrance as the lights went on was the skunk, whose presence could not be mistaken.

One member of the cast had a small-sized piano and Joe played it for twenty minutes between the acts. Students danced in the aisles. He was sensational. He included "The Honeydripper," his hit tune. "Fit to Print" was a huge success.

The college newspaper played it up—that the skunk was the only one who got in to see the play for one scent. The stage crew burned sugar, sprayed the stage and theater with perfume and opened the doors and no one left the building.

Success was a great motivator. Dad couldn't be stopped. The next year he and his friend Harold Otwell wrote "Out on a Limb." The script was well written and performed with much fanfare on the college stage. In 1940, Dad became president of Skull and Dagger. The audience's adulation on the college stage was the foundation of a lifelong love of live theater. He was born for theater; behind the scenes or in the scenes.

11

The World at War

Life on campus continued in 1938 as if all was right with the world. In truth, the world was anything but peaceful. Europe was being forced into war. The rise of Adolf Hitler and the Third Reich in Germany increased the tension and instability throughout Europe. In September 1939, Germany invaded Poland in a bold move to take over Europe. The noose continued to tighten. By 1940 Germany had invaded Norway, Denmark, France, Belgium, Holland and Luxembourg. This became the official start of World War II.

The Axis powers supporting Germany were Italy and Japan. Hitler's Nazi party promoted the idea of an Aryan race; a master race superior to all others. Gays, gypsies, disabled, non-Aryans, and particularly Jews, were persecuted. As Germany gained power, anti-Semitism spread to epidemic proportions. The consequences were grim and relentless. Homes and possessions of Jews were confiscated, families were taken away never to be seen again, shops owned by Jews were at first boycotted, progressing to vandalism and destruction. Executions in the street were daily occurrences.

The United States was far removed from the borders of Europe and tried to remain neutral though England and France had declared war on Germany. The frightening daily newspaper headlines of the escalation was only reported on radio since television production was suspended due to the war.

Both Mom and Dad graduated from college in 1941. Dad received his diploma in February and Mom a semester later in June. They had each earned a Bachelor of Arts degree in Teaching Curricula at the elementary level. A review of Dad's transcript confirmed his strength was definitely in P.E., Drama, and Education. Mom was a better than average student. She also excelled in Drama and received an "A" for a class in Preparation for Marriage. She was ready.

A short time after graduating, Dad received an offer of employment as a full-time teacher for San Diego City Schools. He was assigned to work at the Naval Training School but ended up teaching at Loma Portal Elementary School. The school was merely a few blocks from Mom's family home.

He was assigned to teach sixth grade and lasted just a year before he determined this was not his calling. His career choice of elementary education was short lived. Cocky, midpuberty, six grade boys, were out of control and Dad had a unique method of discipline. Always serving as the pitcher in the softball game during physical education, he aimed the balls a bit closer to the kids then the plate. They quickly got the message. "Gee, Mr. Schultz, that came mighty close to me." "So sorry Joey. That was an accident."

In addition to trying to control raging hormones of twelve-year-old preteens, Dad's entrepreneurial creativity flowed. He invented a game called "Touch Rugby" that he introduced at his school. It combined all the skills and thrills of football, basketball, soccer, and rugby, without the dangers involved in those sports.

In a January, 1942, newspaper column titled "Calling the Shots" George Herrick, San Diego Tribune sports editor, stated "It (Touch Rugby) has all the earmarks of being an excellent preparatory game for major sports, as it emphasizes the basic fundamentals of running, kicking, passing and catching. If Schultz' brain child catches on, it might be we have a genius in our midst. Who says there is nothing new under the sun?" The game was registered and copyrighted at the Library of Congress: Class AA, No. 399809.

The following school year Mom was also hired as an elementary school teacher at Cabrillo Elementary School and it was a much better fit for her. She had a compassionate loving manner with children. She found teaching rewarding and a truly noble profession.

On October 26th, 1941, after dating for four years throughout college, Charlotte Joy Fried, 21 years old, and Sol Schultz, 23 years old, tied the matrimonial knot at 1:00 PM at the Park Manor Hotel. Rabbi Bergman of the large reform Temple Beth Israel performed the ceremony followed by a dinner at the hotel. Bridesmaids and groomsmen were Mom's sisters and Dad's brothers-in-law.

Mom wore her cousin Miriam's wedding dress. The dress was not her choice or style. In fact, she hated it. It was a financial decision since the Fried family was supporting cousin Miriam Oliner through nursing school. Other extended family members in Utah also needed assistance leaving little money for expenditures like a new wedding dress.

The newlyweds took a brief honeymoon reliving their first outing together to the snow in the Laguna Mountains. This time it ended with the car having a cracked engine block. This shaky start was no indication of the happiness to follow.

Mr. & Mrs. Sol Schultz,
October 26, 1941

12

You're in the Army Now

The rumors that leaked out of Europe by 1941 were sensational and horrendous. Germany, after invading multiple countries, hoped to spread the hate of Nazism throughout the world. On December 7, 1941, the United States was stunned by Japanese bombers who launched a surprise and devastating attack on Pearl Harbor, Hawaii. Neutrality was no longer a possibility and the United States entered the fight, now a world war, on the side of the allies.

The newlyweds plans for the future were upended. It was a mere six weeks after Mom and Dad had promised to spend a lifetime together-for better or worse. 'Worse' was heading their way.

On October 5, 1942, three weeks before their first anniversary, an unwanted letter in the form of a draft notice from the Army of the United States was delivered in the mailbox of their rented home. It stated that

1942: Dad with his mother, ready to report for duty

"Special confidence being placed in the integrity and ability of Sol Schultz- he is hereby appointed assistant leader of a contingent of selected men from the local board of San Diego County." Dad was charged with enforcing the Selective Service Regulations governing selected men en route to Induction Stations during the journey from San Diego to Los Angeles, California. He had merely one week to report for duty.

Solomon NMI Schultz, Army Serial Number 39538197, was enlisted as a Private. After his induction at Fort MacArthur, San Pedro, California, on October 16th, 1942, Mom received a Western Union – *"Dearest on my way to Florida will send airmail spec. on arrival miss you love Sol."*

In 1940, Camp Blanding in Starke, Florida, was leased to the United States Army as an active duty training center. From 1940 to 1945, more than 800,000 soldiers received all or part of their training there. During the course of the war, Camp Blanding served as an infantry replacement training center, an induction center, a German prisoner-of-war compound, and a holding center for 343 Japanese, German, and Italian immigrant residents of the United States.

On November 10, 1942, a Western Union telegram sent from Camp Blanding, accurately expressed Dad's homesickness and loneliness. He was missing his "Little Girl." It also alluded to the fact that he found out that Mom was expecting their first child. *"You're wonderful -happiest guy in world- don't ever forget I love you- wait for letter- love Solly."* His letters were filled with romanticism... and lovingly had almost no news

Mom and Dad together at Camp Blanding

of what was happening in the thick of wartime.

In January 1943, a four month pregnant 22½ year old Army wife boarded a Pullman for Jacksonville, Florida, with a stop in New Orleans. She was consumed with morning sickness on the train, the stifling humidity, and the abundance of bugs when she arrived in Florida. This was only tolerable by the knowledge that Dad was waiting for her.

By April 1943 Dad's telegrams included love to Mom and 'baby Mike,' although there was no confirmation of the baby's gender. The telegrams sent in May 1943 included love to 'Charlotte, Mike, and Judy'—just to be on the safe side.

During his physical exam Dad's severe hearing loss was deemed a disability. This may have saved his life since it disqualified him from serving when most of his unit was sent overseas. He remained in Starke and described his post in a letter sent airmail with a six cent stamp on April 1, 1943. *"Well, here am I in Spec. Serv. At the Station Hospital! Some job-the shifts are —clean it up at 8 am. until 8:30-rest until your shift. It alternates 11-2, 2-5, 5-8, 8-11, so it is really ok."* On April 3, 1943 he wrote *"Honey, I hear so many views and things I don't know what to believe but I am tracing them all down and I believe I will know a little more about the end of this month. Nothing much before, I don't think. Still I am lucky to be here and not over there."*

The correspondence on April 4, 1943, just one day later, again confirmed that Dad was a lonely romantic. He penned: *"My Dearest Babypie: Dear, I've decided to love you 1,000,000,000,000 years and then double that because you are the most wonderful wife in all the world. How could anyone help but love you mostest-I do. I am glad you got someone to take your bags and I guess by now you have had a happy reunion with your grand family.... Let's keep praying and God will watch over us and help us. Gee, honey, do you know that Mike (or Judy) will arrive in about 2-2 ½ months. Gosh, I'm getting as excited as if I was having a baby."*

Dad continued his letter with no news. They were filled with nothing but adoration for Mom and a desire to be home. He closes the note....*"Well, dearest, take care of yourself and ------ be careful and we will soon be together again. I love you, hone—Love Me-Your Solly."*

The very next day Dad typed a two page repetitious letter of love again from Camp Blanding with the salutation *"My Dearest darling snuggiepants."* In it he mentioned "Michael Edward" and "Mike" a number of times. *"I sure am excited about Mike. It is awfully sweet of him to send me a kick goodnight— pretty soon maybe a little kiss from his mommie goodnight when she puts him to sleep. But he will probably sleep all the time so his mom will just have to kiss me all the time."*

On May 14, 1943, Dad was honorably discharged from the Army of the United States. For his seven months and eleven days of service, he was given $200 in mustering-out payment for serving more than sixty days, none of which was outside the United States. While his hearing was poor, the cause of the discharge, his character was stated as "Excellent".

13

Michael Edward

Dad was fortunate to make it home in time for the arrival of his firstborn child. Michael Edward officially entered the world in the form of a beautiful baby girl on June 23, 1943, with the war still raging. A fair redhead with light blue eyes just like her Dad, she was named Judith Louise. Judy, at 20 inches and 8 lbs.10 oz. was issued her own War Ration Book by the Office of Price Administration.

Lottie and Morris had purchased a vacant lot in Loma Portal as a wedding gift to Mom and Dad. The anticipation of building a home on the lot was thrilling though 1943, in the midst of a world war, was not the time for this undertaking. Who could consider constructing a new home when everything from gasoline to shoes, from firewood to butter, was rationed? Mom and Dad were just happy to be safely together with their new baby. Now Dad needed to find work. The family of three rented a home on Sterne Street, located a couple of miles away from their vacant lot. They soon moved again to another rental at 1982 Chatsworth Street.

For two more long years World War II raged on many fronts. In May 1945 Germany surrendered, followed shortly thereafter by the surrender of the Japanese in August. The war was the most devastating international conflict in history, taking the lives estimated at sixty million people. Three percent of the world's population had been eliminated. Millions more were injured, and still more lost their homes and property. Much of the world was in a shambles.

It was a particularly emotional time for American Jews. The daily news reported the astounding conditions that European Jews had endured. Stories of death camps, starvation, destruction, and humiliation shocked the world. Particularly painful was the realization that the United States government was unwilling to get involved in helping to save the Jewish population of Europe. Sadly, much of Morris' family had perished, but the Oliner and Schultz families were luckier. Family members had emigrated from Europe well before the war.

Though weary from years of sacrifice, Americans found a reason to feel positive for the first time in years. Optimism in the country spread during the summer of 1945. Increased birth rates months later were indicative of this. The new generation was coined "baby boomers."

Now that the war was over, Mom and Dad were anxious to build their dream home on their gifted lot. Dad was looking for a steady job and finances were tight when Mom approached him. "Sol, Mama and Daddy say we can move in with them while the house is being built. It will save us so much money. That'll really give us a chance to get ahead. What do you think?" Dad wasn't enthralled with the idea of living with his in-laws, though he was very fond of them. But the plan made economic sense.

Lottie and Morris generously welcomed the family into 3436 Elliott Street. They knew this would give the young couple a financial boost. They had confidence in Dad's ability to find work cognizant of his ambition, drive, and work ethic. So they were silent when Dad snapped with crankiness. His short temper flared and he shouted when Morris turned up the heat. "It's too hot in here. I'm boiling." A restless young dad, an inexperienced new mother, and a tiny baby, were a challenge to live with.

Dad considered all possibilities of employment. He was searching for something, but he wasn't sure what that was. He gravitated towards sales, no matter what the product was. This led him to the furniture industry where he tried wholesale, consignment, retail, and liquidation. He had no problem getting a job. Sticking with a job was the challenge. Dad would dive into a new venture and give it his full attention. Once he found success, boredom soon set in and he was no longer interested. If his business wasn't successful, he didn't dwell on that failure. He moved on.

Judy was almost two years old when Mom and Dad were ready to expand their family. Again, Dad was hoping for a son when they sent out the following announcement:

Due to a previously successful adventure
A couple we know are planning expanding
Judy insists that she wants a brother
So Charlotte and Sol are expecting another

In February 1946 they were busy working on their nearly completed home at 3511 Curtis Street. While construction was being completed on the inside, Dad ambitiously set about building a backyard fence. Mom, her cotton maternity blouse draped over her protruding stomach, agreed to assist in holding the fence boards. Dad instructed his very pregnant wife. "Charlotte, hold the fence post steady while I hammer in these nails. Charlotte, can you get me the saw?"

At 8 ½ months along, Mom insisted the extra activity, and a bump in the stomach with a fence board, hastened labor. She gave birth to me two weeks before my projected due date after an afternoon of apprenticeship. I did not possess the Y chromosome Dad had hoped for but XX chromosomes produced a 5 lb 10 oz baby girl born at Mercy Hospital at 1:20 PM on February 25, 1946. I was named Susan Joan and was described in my baby book as having "light brown hair (not much), blue eyes, and fair skin" with a "beautiful" shaped head. Mom calmly said "We're glad we have her" while Dad's diplomatic comment was "I'm glad it's a girl." Over the years my light brown hair turned darkest brown and the blue eyes turned to greenish hazel.

I was reportedly an adventurous night owl who climbed out of my crib at twenty months and walked like a night stalker around the house at all hours. Mom and Dad solved the problem by moving me into a big bed at twenty-two months. They created a "Dutch door" by cutting the bedroom door in half horizontally, leaving the top half open as I was unable to turn the doorknob on the lower half. That solved the problem. I could crawl out of my bed during the night and play on the floor until I fell back to sleep where they would find me in the morning surrounded by toys.

As soon as I could walk, I followed my big sister around. When I began to express myself through my voice, "Huki" was the best I could do to pronounce Judy's name. Her fractured nickname stuck with her. As I got older I created and expanded the moniker, calling her "Hukskidscandedandelorous". She never outgrew the name and is still called "Huki" by the family.

Me and my big sister, "Huki"

Childhood Memories

Playing on our backyard swings & in our playhouse
Dressing my dolls with wardrobes Mom created
Our pet frogs and dogs
Summer days at Ocean Beach
Taking road trips with Nanny & Morris Daddy
Our house full of friends
Mom teaching me to sew
Visits from my Los Angeles cousins
Days turning into weeks, months, years; happy and carefree

This was my childhood.
I was part of a close, loving family. I was one cog in the wheel.
Each of us essential- the whole greater than the sum of its parts.
Unconditional love and unwavering support.
Feeling like I was perfect in my Mother's eyes.

14

Our House Becomes Our Home

Our new house on Curtis Street was a one story angular style popular post World War II. The neat row of homes on both sides of the street were dwarfed by large two story structures on three corners. Our location was just a few short blocks from Loma Portal Elementary School where Dad began

The house Mom & Dad built at 3911 Curtis Street

and ended his teaching career. The best thing from Mom's vantage point was the close proximity to the white Spanish style house with the red tile roof where she lived from the age of twelve with her two sisters and where her parents, my Nanny and Morris Daddy, still lived.

Our cracker box dwelling was complete with two bedrooms, a den, and one central bathroom. A narrow hallway, connecting the bedrooms to the living area, was just wide enough for me to practice my monkey climb. I found I could press one hand and one foot on either side of the hall walls, straddle the space between, and crawl the length of the hallway at two feet in the air. Smudge prints formed abstract art along the Navajo White walls. Like his father years before, who had yelled about the cost of repapering the walls, Dad's voice could be heard in exasperation, "Susie, will you stop climbing the walls? I can't paint them every few months to cover up your dirty handprints and footprints."

The names of authors: Alcott, Browning, Curtis, Dumas, etc., were used alphabetically to designate the Loma Portal streets. At each intersection a tall post rose from a cement pedestal. A glass globe covered a light bulb that lit the street in the evening. One afternoon when everything became too quiet, Mom went to check up on me, a five year old who often role played for hours as a doting mother of my plastic and rubber baby dolls. She searched each room of the house and the yard with no success. "Susie, Susie, where are you?" Mom's voice became louder and edged with anxiety. In desperation she reached the front door, turned the handle and hurried down three steps to the walkway.

There I was sitting happily on the cement pedestal in the intersection. I was mothering my dolls, cuddling and dressing them. Drivers carefully maneuvered around the lamppost doing a double take at the little girl unaware of danger. In a swift move, Mom ran out and scooped me up. The three or so swats on my bottom shocked me to tears. I was rarely scolded and had never been spanked before. I understood from that day on, that streetlights were off-limits for play. The impact of my punishment remained. This was my first and only spanking.

Even after its initial completion, the Curtis street house was in a constant state of construction. With a sense of pride, Dad moved from project to project: upgrading, renovating, and adding on to his castle. The list of improvements was endless. Family rooms had become popular so one was added. When master bathrooms became popular, Dad contracted for one. A small room was built onto the master bedroom for dual use; as an office for Dad and a sewing room for Mom

Besides these home improvements, Dad's hobby was leathercrafting. Special tools were used to carve intricate patterns of flowers onto stiff shiny natural hides. The embellished pieces were laced together to create handbags that were popular at the time. This creative outlet did nothing to quell Dad's restlessness. His brain was perennially in motion and he possessed endless energy.

Dad and his brother, Jack, decided to go into business together. They opened up Schultz' Furniture. After a brief time, for reasons unknown, the store closed. The excellent location between B & C Street in downtown San Diego later became the home of the San Diego Civic Center.

Though confirmation is not possible, McSchultz Furniture may have been Dad's next enterprise, or maybe there were a few ventures in between. This discount store was located at 6th and University, in the heart of the Hillcrest area of San Diego. Furniture was sold from a Quonset hut, a lightweight prefabricated structure of corrugated galvanized steel.

The half sphere shaped Quonset hut did not resemble anything permanent or classy though it was a fitting design for McSchultz Furniture. The store with filled with goods supplied by Burnett Furniture, a large retail store carrying name brand furniture located nearby at 7th and University. Slow moving merchandise was moved to McSchultz Furniture on consignment and sold at discounted prices. Dad had found a good niche market.

In 1992, many decades after Dad's foray into the furniture business, The San Diego Union published an article about Jerome's Furniture, still a fixture in San Diego today. The article was titled "The Making of a Furniture Man" and began with a quote by current owner Jerry Navarra. "The concept was simple. Sell quality furniture at discount prices. And sell it in a warehouse atmosphere...The concept was new in 1954, but it worked. It continues to work for Jerome's Furniture, now approaching its 38th year in the San Diego market. This concept was the brainchild of Vincent Jim Navarra, Sol Schultz and Alexander Strep." Jerome's Furniture continues to follow the 65 year old business plan today.

Society's image of the perfect family in the 1950s was narrow. The man of the family was expected to be the breadwinner, providing the major financial support. A woman's role was to take care of the house, the meals, and the children. She was to greet her working spouse after a hard day at the office perfectly coiffed with a smile, a drink, and the aroma of a home cooked meal drifting from the kitchen.

But Mom and Dad never followed convention. Mom did not spend much time in the kitchen and Dad didn't drink. Dad charged forward, zig-zagged between employment, self-employment, and unemployment while Mom provided unwavering support. We learned how to decode when money was tight. When Dad was out of work or started a new venture, Mom stepped in to help pay the bills with her fallback career as a teacher.

In the early 1950's, March 1st was the cutoff date for children to enter kindergarten. Any child who turned five years old after that date entered school the following September. My February birthday made it a requirement that I start school at the tender age of 4 ½. I was not only very small, I wasn't ready to leave the 'nest'. My first day of kindergarten was a memorable one. I was so afraid to ask my teacher, Mrs. Smith, if I could go to the bathroom I wet my pants - twice.

Mom was working as a long term substitute teacher that year so Dad was responsible for getting me and Judy to school. After school one day Mrs. Smith called home. "Mrs. Schultz, I'd like to ask you who is dressing Susie in the morning for school?" Mom answered hesitantly "When I go to teach, Sol gets Susie dressed. Why do you ask?" Mrs. Smith paused "I really hate to mention it, but she had her dress on backwards again today. The buttons were in the front instead of the back."

Mom didn't complain about returning to teach, at least not to us. She never lost faith in Dad. Whether he was successful or not, she was the perennial optimist and he was the go-getter.

Often Dad told us stories of his disadvantaged childhood: especially bathing in the washtub, walking to school alone, and enduring the outdoor toilet. I was empathetic to Dad's suffering. "I'm so glad you came to live with us Daddy. Everything is better in our house."

Mom and Dad had hoped for a large family. They had already defied the odds and the doctors who had informed Mom after a bout with mumps in her early twenties that she would be unable to conceive children. After the birth of two daughters they were confident they would be blessed with more children. But in the years that followed, their desire for more children was preempted by the multiple miscarriages Mom suffered. After the last miscarriage Dad arrived home from the hospital, his face long and drawn. "I'm so sorry to tell you that Mom lost our baby....I guess we will have to get a puppy instead of a baby brother or sister." Our family was completed with the addition of a puppy.

Judy was in the first grade when she contracted Scarlet Fever. Scarlet Fever affected children from ages five to fifteen and was highly contagious. Symptoms included a sore throat, fever, and a rash. On notification, the Public Health Department posted a "Quarantined" sign on the front door of our house. Judy was secluded in Mom and Dad's bedroom and Mom, wearing a mask, was the only one able to tend to her. All her toys were thrown out to prevent the disease from spreading. Dad stayed with Nanny and Morris Daddy and I stayed in the house with Mom, though far away from my sister.

After a couple of weeks she was over the contagious period. Mom, Nanny, Judy, and I went to the corner drug store in Ocean Beach for lunch to celebrate. It was a short-lived celebration. Judy came home with a fever and new diagnosis of German measles. She was home from school for another two weeks.

My own health was a concern a few years later when I was about eight years old. During a routine check-up the doctor had detected a heart murmur leading to a summer filled with various doctor's ap-

Quarantined when Judy had Scarlett Fever

pointments. During one of the last appointments, my anxious mother escorted me to the pediatric cardiologist's office. I sat, bare-chested, with my feet dangling from the examining table that faced the second floor window. I stared down at the tops of cars whizzing by on the street below. The cold stethoscope bell was pressed against my pale chest. The doctor leaned in towards me with his head down. "Take a deep breath now. Keep going. Take another one. Breathe out slowly," he directed as he moved the metal circle from spot to spot. After this appointment I was diagnosed with a "functional" heart murmur. I was just glad for this trying summer to end. Mom was relieved, but not for long.

Following my health scare, in 1952, a very serious epidemic consumed the country with fear. The disease, Paralytic Poliomyelitis, known as "polio," paralyzed the body. This crippling illness was considered to be spread through sanitation habits. Thus, community pools were closed and children were kept away from crowds. Throughout that summer mothers scrambled to entertain children with quiet indoor activities. Each week new cases of polio were diagnosed. There was no indication where or when polio would strike. I arrived home from school one day to hear frightening news. "I just heard that your friend, Karen, has polio. They don't know how serious it is yet. I am just sick about it." Mom's voice reflected anguish. The next week another schoolmate became infected with polio. The results were scary as news spread of people crippled, only able to survive in an iron lung. Thankfully, in 1955 scientist Jonas Salk discovered the first successful polio vaccine and parents rushed to have their children vaccinated against this horrific disease.

When Dad was working, Mom's involvement in our lives reconfirmed that we were most important and her highest priority. She chauffeured us to ballet, ice skating, tennis, served as a Girl Scout leader, and was active in the PTA. I still expected her to be home when I arrived after school, to inquire about my day while readying a snack. She never disappointed me.

While we were at school she tended to her own activities: volunteer work, a weekly game of bridge or a rummy game called Pan. Her sewing club met monthly to display their projects, share family updates, and gossip. The Potluck group, six couples who had been friends before any of them had children, met for dinner each month.

Loma Portal Elementary School included grades K-6. At the end of third grade I decided to run for the office of Student Body Secretary. The term would begin the following school year when I would be in the fourth grade. I gave a short speech during the school assembly. "I will work hard if I am elected Student Body Secretary and I will use my best handwriting to take minutes. Vote for me, Susie Schultz." I had no platform or policies to promote and I actually had little interest in student government. What was exciting about this position was getting to sit on the stage during school assemblies every couple of weeks, read the minutes of the past assembly aloud, and take a written record of the current gathering. When the winners were announced, my name was called. I couldn't wait for the first assembly in September.

My excitement soon fizzled. The first school assembly was scheduled on Yom Kippur, the holiest day of the year in the Jewish religion. Yom Kippur is a day of reflection, declaring and admitting to past sins, fasting throughout the day and asking for redemption from God. It is also one of two days a year that our family always attended religious services at Temple Beth Israel. It was to be a day we put on our best dresses, joined with other Jewish families, and cleared our minds of daily mundane things. On this important day, the end of a ten-day period called the Days of Awe, we were to ask God to "Inscribe us in the Book of Life" for the new year. No matter what our sins were, "Penitence, prayer, and charity," could avert the result. This was quite visual to me and I wanted to be around for the next year!

But I was upset and angry. *Wouldn't God understand how important this was?* "Of all the days of the year, why does the assembly have to fall on this day? I don't want to go to Temple. I don't like it. It's too long," I whined. Mom and Dad paused "Susie, this is the holiest day of the year. This is a day to stop and think about what you have done this past year and how you can be a better person. Think about that. Are you ashamed to tell the Principal you are Jewish and that this is a holy day and it's why you won't be there?"

I sulked with arms defiantly crossed in front of my chest. Mom sat down beside me. "Do what you think is right. If you think it is more important to go to the assembly, then go ahead. You make the decision." And I did. The morning of the assembly I got on my favorite dress, gathered my notebook with the minutes I had carefully copied in my best cursive, and headed out the door. I walked about a block and a half from home when I could go no further. I stopped, briefly hesitated, turned around, walked home, and joined the family for the ride to Temple Beth Israel.

I never could explain how I made the decision to turn back. Was it Jewish guilt or the values Mom and Dad had instilled in me at a tender age of eight? The day remains clear and crisp in my mind's eye. Mom and Dad had the courage to give me the choice.

15

Sundays Visits

Encouraged and prodded by Mom, many of our Sunday afternoons were spent visiting Dad's parents. He parked the car in the narrow driveway. Upon entering the house, the dark living room and stale smell of cigarette smoke overwhelmed us. Grandpa Louis, whose continuous cough and fingers were stained from nicotine, was a handsome man whose silver hair was neatly parted on the side and combed down. He wore a dark colored bathrobe covering his frail body. He was partially reclining in his oversized chair by the window while sitting on his "donut" to ease his pain from rectal cancer.

Grandma Anna, her gray hair pulled back in a bun, and wearing a housedress covered by a well-worn apron, welcomed the family. Grandma gave us a hug at the same time she pulled a treat out of her apron pocket. "Here. For you. Juicy Fruit chewing gum." The obligatory Sunday visit would last a couple of hours until there was nothing left to say.

This tradition began when Judy was an infant, long before I was born. On one Sunday visit Dad playfully tossed baby Judy in the air. Thrown a bit too energetically, she grazed the ceiling. Dad recalled vividly "Judy was fine but I thought my dad was going to kill me when he saw that."

Occasionally, on a Sunday evening, Dad, Mom, and infant Judy were invited to dinner. Usually a boiled chicken was served. One night as the family gathered around the kitchen table for dinner, Judy began to cry. Mom left the table and retrieved a bottle filled with warm milk to feed her hungry baby. Grandma stared, her eyes wide open. What she had witnessed made her speechless. "Mein Gott," she whispered under her breath, "She's giving her milk at the table. We are having chicken."

Mom was unaware that she had broken a forbidden religious law, one of the 613 commandments in the Torah. Mom had committed an unforgivable offense. She had served milk at the same meal that meat was being served. The consequences for her faux pas were long-lasting. She was given a life sentence. The Jewish girl from Ashton, Idaho, a girl who attended the Methodist Church with friends, never received another dinner invitation from Ma and Pa.

Grandma lived into her mid 90's, outliving her teeth by many years. She never had dentures, preferring to exist with merely two teeth readily displayed when she smiled.

16

Nanny & Morris Daddy

Mom's parents, our Nanny and Morris Daddy, anchored us. They confirmed a feeling of love by the pleasure they expressed when we were in their company.

Jack LaLanne, known as "The Godfather of Modern Fitness," hosted an exercise show on television from 1953 to 1985. He preached exercise and a healthy diet. Morris Daddy didn't need 'The Godfather' to encourage him. He was his own fitness and nutrition guru, spreading the message of health through vitamins, fruits, vegetables, and exercise, to anyone who would listen. His slight physique showed no muscle mass, though each day he took a long brisk walk around the neighborhood.

Like the marathon runner who breaks to hydrate with a cup of water, his walk always included a stop at our Curtis Street house. He would switch from exercising his body to exercising his mind. His early morning arrival usually coincided with Mom at the breakfast table enjoying her morning tea. While walking, he thought about current events and world news or an interesting article he wanted to share. By the time he arrived at the door he was ready for a give-and-take and Mom was more than willing to hear his opinions and express hers.

One day in 1956 he broached a topic that baffled him.

"Charlotte dear, I saw that dark-haired boy from Memphis on the Ed Sullivan Show last night. I couldn't believe the way he moved and the loud music. The girls in the audience were screaming and crying. Can you explain what they were screaming about?" "Daddy, that's Elvis Presley. All the girls, including Judy and Susie, are crazy about him." With his hands poised on his narrow hips, he let out a high-pitched giggle "Ho, ho, ho. Is that so? You don't say? I don't understand it." His slight body shook with laughter.

Nanny ignored Morris Daddy's focus on nutrition. Exercise and carrot juice were of no interest to her. But her sweet personality was boosted by her active sweet tooth.

Judy and I often stayed over on Saturday night when Mom and Dad went out for the evening. "Girls, how about playing some Canasta?" Nanny would suggest when we arrived. They taught us how to count the points to meld and how to make a Canasta on the gray and white Formica table in the alcove off the kitchen. Midway through the game Morris Daddy cut two pears up into quarters and placed one bowl next to each of us on the table while advertising their virtues. "Girls, you need to eat pears. They contain so many nutrients like vitamin C to keep you healthy."

Nanny, standing behind Morris Daddy, rolled her eyes and twirled her index finger at her temple gesturing "crazy person." She followed up the lecture and pears by presenting a glossy white box we knew all too well. "Now girls, help yourselves to our favorite - See's Candy." We were so familiar with the shapes and markings on the top of each piece we readily dug in to those with the fillings we preferred. For the few pieces that were unidentifiable we would gently push a thumb into the underside of the chocolate to peek inside. If it didn't look appealing, we would carefully put it back in the pleated brown candy cup and gently place it back in the box.

17

"I Need Space"

"I don't want to share a room with her anymore. Susie has her dolls and doll stuff all over the place. I want my own room!" Judy begged until Mom and Dad found a way to alter our small house and give Judy her distance - away from me. The front porch was enclosed, adding square footage to the small den making the space into a suitable bedroom. The only drawback was that the garage could only be accessed from the interior of the house through Judy's new bedroom and her makeshift closet. "Dad, you did it again! You left the door to the garage open!" Judy was exasperated and she let Dad know it each and every time he forgot to secure the door. It didn't bother her that the new bedroom had a large window that faced the front exterior of the house. This exit became very convenient for Judy as a teenager; giving her an easy way to sneak out of the house at night.

While Dad was out searching San Diego for business opportunities, he left Mom to quietly lead us through our teenage years by the guidelines in her own internal How to Parent manual. She had a solid theory that she lived by. "If it isn't harmful or hurtful, it doesn't matter. Save it for the important things." She shared her motto with her friends who refused to allow their teens to follow current but silly fads. On the contrary, she allowed me to get my long ponytail cut into a popular, though unattractive, brush-up, while my lips were coated with the current craze of ghost white lipstick. At age 13, Mom supported me when I chose to change the spelling of my nickname to 'Suzi'. She was cognizant that these were not the important things.

The newly added family room on Curtis Street became a hangout for our dance parties and evening get-togethers. Summer days were spent at the beach and on warm summer nights we played tennis on the nearby high school courts until it was too dark to see the balls. As soon as the sun dropped below the horizon, whoever had played would amble two blocks to our house.

Small vinyl records, 45 RPMs, containing a single song, had become popular. We stacked them up on the adapter of our record player. One by one they dropped down, the arm swung over, and the needle moved to the outside groove of the vinyl. We mouthed the words of the top tunes along with our favorite heartthrobs. "Dre-e-e-am, dream, dream, dream," the smooth sound of the Everly Brothers became the background to our snacking, chatting, and flirting. We had not a care in the world.

B-a-n-g-b-a-n-g-b-a-n-g. We heard a loud angry knock at the door about nine o'clock one night. Dad opened the door to find our neighbor, Mr. Zimmerman, with a scowl on his face. He shouted above the music, "Those kids need to turn that damn music down and keep quiet. I am fed up with their music and all the noise that's going on every night this summer." Dad exploded, "These kids aren't doing anything but having fun. They're welcome here and they can dance and play their music as loud as they want. You better go back home or I'll knock your block off," he threatened. Mr. Zimmerman hesitated, thought better of a response, and timidly turned and left. From that day forward, Mr. and Mrs. Zimmerman avoided us. Dad, whose bark was much bigger than his bite, never hit anyone before, during, or after this incident.

"Girls, you aren't allowed to have any boys in the house when we aren't home." Mom and Dad emphasized one of the few rules we had.

One Saturday night we were home alone after Mom and Dad left for an evening out with friends. The car cruised down the street just as Judy's boyfriend, Bill, arrived at the door. Of course we let him in the house, ignoring our strict house rule. A few minutes later we heard the car in the driveway. Mom had forgotten something and they had returned back home to retrieve it. When Dad opened the front door, he caught a glimpse of Bill as he ran into the bathroom, shut the door, and climbed out the small high window. Dad was fuming. In an angry voice he turned to Judy, "Did you have any boys in the house, Judy?" Her blue eyes looked up to his blue eyes and she replied adamantly "NO!" There was a pause and Dad turned to me, "Suzi, were there any boys in the house?" I hesitated. Then my bottom lip began to tremble and I started to cry. Dad went running out the front door hoping to catch the speedy teen half his age. Though he wasn't caught, I don't recall Bill ever gracing our house again.

Mom drummed into our psyche consequences of wayward teens who had been swayed by their emotions and momentary passion. "Poor Judge Thomas. His daughter, Barbara, got pregnant and she had to quit school. You know Marge, from the sewing group? Her niece left school in her senior year to live with her aunt far away and had a baby she gave up for adoption. What a hard thing for the whole family."

My knowledge of sex in my coming-of-age years was minimal at best. Sex Education class was part of our school curriculum covering basic anatomy. Female and male reproductive illustrations were clinical. The movie showing a birth was frankly frightening. During the question and answer portion of class the teacher, in a matter-of-fact manner, commented "You can even get pregnant with your clothes on by sitting on a boy's lap." If that wasn't scary enough, the stories of unwanted pregnancy and illegal abortions in back alleys, performed with a rusty coat hanger often leading to death, were effective deterrents.

Me & Huki coming-of-age

18

The Jewish Community: Post World War II

The horrors of World War II affected all Americans but especially the Jewish population. The Holocaust had claimed the lives of twelve million people, six million of them Jews. Over half a million Jews had served in the United States Armed Forces over the course of the war and most Americans felt sympathetic towards Jewish refugees. Organizations that had provided services to Jews were more motivated than ever to assist displaced persons and survivors. The Joint Distribution Committee and United Jewish Federation (UJF) were active non-profit organizations that solicited funds for local purposes and for Israel and Jewish communities throughout the world.

Mom and many of her close friends were avid supporters of UJF, both with their time and money. In 1946 a Women's Division of UJF was developed independent of the Men's Division. Women making monetary commitments in their own name was a novel idea for the times. Each year Mom was provided a list of friends and acquaintances to contact requesting financial support.

Shopping in the mall one day in the late 1950s, Mom and I met a woman who was on her list of potential donors. Mom greeted Carol with a friendly smile and began making small talk. "Hi Carol, you look great. How are you? Suzi and I have been having fun shopping for school clothes. What are you looking for?" The conversation continued until Mom felt the superficial chatter had gone on long enough. Like a bee diving for nectar from the heart of a flower in the spring she asked directly, "By the way Carol, you are on my list for a pledge this year for UJF. You know this year we need your support more than ever....." she continued enthusiastically to list the many needs of refugees locally and overseas.

To put it mildly, I was embarrassed. I looked the other way, pretending to browse the store windows while Mom continued her pitch. But Carol didn't appear offended. She made her verbal commitment with a smile. Mom thanked her and the two women said their good-byes. We walked away and Mom turned to me, "Suzi, you don't have to be uncomfortable or ashamed of me for asking for a donation. After all, there are so many people who need our help. I am not asking for myself."

Possibly in sympathy, American Jews began to experience a new level of acceptance. At the same time, the reform movement led many Jews to downplay religious traditions. We did our best to defy the stereotypes. We had our noses shortened, gave more than our fair share to charitable causes, displayed vocal and financial support for other minorities, and did our best to fit in. In our own community we wanted to demonstrate we were no different than our neighbors. We tried to be more generous, more caring, and more supportive of social justice. It may have been about assimilating or maybe we were just trying to protect ourselves in case anti-semitism reared its ugly head again.

Temple Beth Israel was the largest reform temple in San Diego. Judy and I attended Sunday School and in the 10th grade a confirmation ceremony affirmed our commitment to Judaism. Our Reform services had little tradition. Hebrew was limited to a few fundamental prayers. We did not regularly attend services though we never missed the Jewish High Holidays: Rosh Hashanah, the beginning of the Jewish New Year, and Yom Kippur, the Day of Atonement, as well as the anniversary of the passing of Mom and Dad's parents. Once a year Judy and I invited our teachers to join us at the annual Friday night religious service honoring educators. We were basically cultural Jews, proud but untethered by rules and traditions.

Our politically conservative community was primarily comprised of "old" San Diego upper middle class Protestant families, and Portuguese Catholic tuna fisherman. Old San Diego families had the status, and the fisherman who owned fishing boats had the wealth. The offspring of the socially accepted families were invited to join Cotillion and Debutantes, a traditional rite-of-passage into the social scene. I was not invited, though the exclusion meant nothing to me at the time.

Surprisingly, the pendulum of anti-Semitism was already swinging back by the late 1950s and early 1960s, a mere decade after the war. The civil rights movement was in the forefront but there was already an underlying knowledge and acceptance of anti-Jewish sentiment in some areas of our fair city.

La Jolla (meaning 'the Jewel' in Spanish), ten miles north of downtown, was the most exclusive and expensive housing area of San Diego. While Point Loma had a handful of Jewish families, La Jolla's Jewish population was non-existent. The local newspaper, The La Jolla Light, wrote the following. "There are, clear, substantiated and well-recorded accounts that point firmly to a virulent culture of housing discrimination in La Jolla aimed primarily at Jews. Real estate agents from that time admit, with a hearty disgust borne from years of keeping a dirty secret, there was a widespread policy of discriminating against Jews searching for houses in La Jolla. Some of the first Jewish settlers in La Jolla remember the distrust they faced and the difficulties they had to overcome in finding an agent who would rent or sell them a house."

This was all about to change with the construction of the respected university in La Jolla, the University of California at San Diego. The gentleman's agreement against housing Jews could no longer be maintained. According to The San Diego Union Tribune, Roger Revelle, the scientist who championed the establishment of UC San Diego stated: "You can have a university or an anti-Semitic covenant. You can't have both. They had some trouble attracting Jewish professors in the beginning. They had heard about La Jolla."

To gauge local attitudes, four Jewish professors who were new to the campus made an agreement. One would apply for membership at the private La Jolla Beach & Tennis Club. "They thought if he could get into the club, no problem," The professor was accepted. No problem. This opened the doors of La Jolla to the Jewish population and other ethnic groups.

19

Jack of all Trades

Dad's variety of jobs led him through a virtual maze. Involved in a smorgasbord of businesses he navigated the challenges, threw himself into every new project and charged on with passion. From teacher to auctioneer to business owner to entrepreneur, he was ready and willing to attempt anything within reason. He led with a positive attitude; anticipating success.

But what Dad actually did do to put food on our table and provide financial support was a wonder to Judy and me. Part of the difficulty was that he constantly changed his line of work. This presented a problem to us. We knew that Paula's dad was a doctor and Claudia's dad was a banker. We struggled to answer when friends inquired, "What does your dad do?" *How should we answer that?* "Oh, he owns a furniture store." "Oh, he bought some washers and dryers to sell." "Oh, he is fixing up an apartment building." We responded with whatever we overheard Mom and Dad discussing and sometimes we just created and embellished whatever was in our youthful minds. We would complete the blank line on the school registration form inquiring "Father's Occupation" with "Housewife" in hopes that administrators would think we got confused and filled in the space incorrectly.

One thing was certain-Dad did love a deal. He attained his auctioneer's license and proceeded to liquidate the assets of failing businesses. With each lot of merchandise he acquired, he arrived home full of excitement. "Charlotte, Huki, Suzi, you aren't going to guess what I did today?" We could predict Dad had scooped up the entire inventory of a sinking retail establishment. Which one was always the mystery.

Dad would burst open the back door and call us all into the kitchen. "I have a fun surprise for you girls! I bought a western store full of cowboy gear. I am putting it up for auction soon so I want you girls and Mom to go pick out whatever you want. There are boots, hats, western shirts, and lots of other neat stuff."

Dad was a true salesman. He saw potential profit in every lot of goods. "You aren't going to believe it. I got a great deal on a lingerie store. You girls are gonna have fun. You need to come down to the store and pick out what you want." After Dad unlocked the building, he left us to try on lacy, sexy bras, underwear, and other exotic lingerie. We loaded bags with 'brothel worthy' garter belts and bikini underpants. We each took Merry Widows, a type of corset commonly worn in the mid 1950s, though they remained in our drawers unworn for years.

We never had any idea whether Dad's liquidation sales were lucrative or not though when Mom periodically went back to substitute teaching it was a good indication of our family's financial situation. Successful or not, Dad moved on from one investment to the next. If the current one failed he was hopeful that the next deal would be a winner.

Dad opened California Warehouse Sales on Market Street. It was two blocks from the Bohemian Bakery, a popular Jewish deli.

Selling appliances did not satisfy Dad's quest for fulfillment and in a short time he was itching to move on. At the age of 39 Dad sold the furniture/ appliance store. With the profit from the store, and help from his in-laws, he  took a plunge into the real estate market. It was risky when he signed the final documents to buy the Sumner Apartments. He had no idea what was involved in being a landlord. The old three story apartment building in downtown San Diego consisted of a few dozen rental units with years of deferred maintenance and much needed renovation.

"I'm just a schlepper in the basement" Dad referred to himself as he began the immense refurbishment. He had proven to be pretty handy at the Curtis Street house, though these outmoded apartments required more than just handyman skills. Dad was not disheartened. With little outside help he charged ahead by trial and error. He had a clear vision and high hopes for this rundown structure that needed everything. It required more than a facelift. Major remodeling, updating, repairs, and cosmetic improvements were in order to bring the Sumner up to its market potential. Dad was up for the challenge.

He spent every weekday for the next year at the Sumner Apartments. He came home each evening covered in dried sweat and sawdust. Often he would drag in an antique table, gilded mirror, or chest of drawers. Every item had wobbly legs and peeling paint. Even the carved wood frame surrounding the scratched mirrors was missing pieces. Dad exclaimed lovingly, "Wouldya look at this beautiful old table? All it needs is a little sanding, staining and a few screws tightened to make

it a perfect addition for our house. Where should we put it?"
He was his own man, on his own terms, and he was happy.
After a year of work, the units were ready and rented. He was
now a landlord. He had found his calling.

20

Lessons

Dad was expecting 'Mike' when Judy arrived, and 'Mike' again when I arrived. He must have anticipated playing softball, coaching Little League, and passing on the intricacies of wrestling to a mini version of himself. Mom might have anticipated we would excel in gymnastics as she did. But that was before they became the parents of two daughters of average athletic ability. Throughout our childhood we were introduced and given unlimited opportunities to a variety of lessons.

My lack of gracefulness was already evident at five years old. Mom enrolled me in ballet classes at Gladys Bowen's Dance Studio. After a series of lessons, my class of costumed little girls were to showcase our progress at our first recital. Mom, Dad, and Judy, came to witness the performance. We tiny ballerinas were to enter the room by walking down the stairs, wearing our crisp tutus resting at our hips over powder pink leotards. We lined up by height, the shortest in front, that meant I was at the beginning of the queue. "Don't forget to smile girls," Mrs. Bowen, the stern studio owner reminded us as she urged the line forward. I took the first step forward, then tripped and tumbled down, as the ballerinas piled up behind me. Tears erupted, though the only lasting result was my short lived vocation as a prima ballerina.

One day Dad took Judy and me bowling. I was twelve years old and weighed about seventy-five pounds. Judy, two and a half years older, took her turn first and, in respectable form, took a few steps towards the pins, then let the ball go. It rolled easily right down the center of the lane. Each revolution brought the ball closer to the headpin. The ball veered slightly as eight of the pins toppled on their side. Dad cheered her on. "Great job, Huki. Two more pins and you would have had a strike. Now go again and knock the others down for a spare." She definitely had potential.

Then it was my turn. In an authoritative voice, Dad gave me instructions. "Okay baby, here's how you do it. Three steps, thumb up, bend your knee, and roll the ball straight down." "Okay, I got it," I confidently replied. I could barely lift the ball, let alone display a presentable form. Doing my best, I stood tall, took three steps, dropped the heavy sphere with a *clunk* on the wooden lane. *Th-u-u-d.....*It slowly, gently, rolled a few feet before curving to the left and dropping into the gutter, doing no harm to the ten upright pins. "Don't worry. Try it again. Now do just what I say," Dad's voice was now elevated. I struggled to lift the ball when it returned. Again I took the three steps forward and dropped the ball on the hardwood lane. It calmly rolled a few feet aiming directly at the pins, then made its way to the gutter. After three attempts to get the huge shiny black and green marbled ball to roll straight, Dad's frustration had reached a limit.

He approached the bowling center manager. "I need your help. I'm trying to teach my youngest daughter how to bowl. She's a lefty with a hook and I don't know what to tell her to fix it." The manager strolled over to our lane and demonstrated the correct technique. "It's easy. Keep your hand straight, swing your arm back, and lean in. Then let her go."

With determination I attempted to correct my form

again. We all stood and stared at the glossy sphere reached its destination in the gutter. When my total score for the game tallied less than Dad's age, he finally gave up.

The half inch scar above my lip covering my right eye tooth reconfirmed that I had more determination than skill when it came to sports. I had just returned from a week at 6th grade camp when a few neighborhood kids joined together to play softball in front of our house. It was a warm, sunny, San Diego spring day and it was Tommy's turn to be the pitcher. "Okay, ready for the pitch?" Tommy leaned in on our homemade pitcher's mound in the middle of the street. It was my turn to bat. The ball rapidly left his hand arching through the air towards me and the angled bat resting on my left shoulder.

T-h-w-a-c-k....Either the pitch was poor, my near-sightedness affected my swing, or my lack of athletic ability was to blame. Either the ball or the bat, I can't remember which, connected above my upper lip. Blood dripped down my chin as I covered my mouth with a dirty hand. "Mom, Mom," I yelled as the kids followed me and the drips of blood on the cement. I was the Pied Piper leading the mice. Mom calmly studied the damage. "I need to call Dr. Mike." She dialed Doctor Mike's number while she held a clean rag against my bloody face. I applied pressure against the rag ignoring the blood stains all over my blouse as we drove to National City where Dr. Mike had his medical office.

Dr. Mike lived across the street and served as our personal physician. Mike and his wife, Ruth, were Mom and Dad's best friends. We arrived at the office and Dr. Mike's nurse, old Mrs. Stiever, called me into a patient room. Five stitches later Mom drove me home with my badge of courage and a lifelong memory of childhood softball games.

While it was very convenient having a family doctor right across the street for emergencies, we weren't always delighted with his generous gifts. The good doctor brought home the most up-to-date injections including polio and flu shots, for his own three daughters and for us. I was not appreciative of these presents.

Tennis was a natural fit for San Diego's climate. Mom and Dad enjoyed social tennis weekly at the Town and Country Club, a membership club that opened in the late 1950s in the developing Mission Valley. Mom signed me up for tennis lessons with Ben Press who taught at the Kona Kai Club on Shelter Island. Coach Press was a stocky energetic man with a head full of curly black hair and a ready smile. He was encouraging and told Mom "Suzi has a lot of potential. She's a lefty like me and that's great. Left-handed players are usually better players than right-handed players once they learn to control the racquet." I liked tennis, but I never practiced enough to learn to control the racquet.

While Mom and Dad played tennis, Judy and I swam in the Olympic sized swimming pool at the Town and Country. Our delight splashing around in the blue chlorinated water was not shared by Dad. He had never learned to swim as a child and

felt fearful and uncomfortable in the water. The extent of his encounter in the pool was to cool off in the shallow end with all the small children.

Due to Mom's insistence, Dad, at the age of 44, reluctantly agreed to take swimming lessons. "Okay, okay. I'll do it. Sign me up." His favorite pastime was deep sea fishing. He thoroughly enjoyed joining a chartered boat for a half day fishing excursion.

Dad loved to go fishing

Occasionally he was invited for a day of fishing on a friend's private boat. Mom threatened "Sol, you are not allowed to go fishing unless you learn to swim. It is just plain dangerous. I love you too much to let you go out in the ocean without being water safe. I don't want you to drown."

The adult swim class was held at the Turquoise Swim School in Mission Valley. On the first day of class Dad entered the Men's locker room and changed into his swim trunks. His muscular physique was freckled and pale in contrast to his tan face and trucker's tan forearms. He gingerly walked to the edge of the pool stepped down in to the turquoise water. He was relieved. *Whew, I can touch the bottom here in the shallow end. It's not so bad.* He made his way over to the Beginning Swimming instructor, a pretty young lady he noted. She was surrounded by a cluster of eleven students. All women.

The next few weeks he did his best to master the breast stroke, the back stroke, and the side stroke, in addition to breathing while attempting the correct aquatic form. After each lesson he would return home revealing that day's class activities. "The instructor showed us how to breathe while swimming today. She said, breathe only through your mouth. Inhale deeply, air that is, and exhale as you would whistle at a girl or blow out candles." Then Dad relayed the assigned homework. "At the end of the class she encouraged us to practice in the tub at home. Inhale and exhale in the water. Turn your head from the left side to face down. I told the teacher that I couldn't practice. I only take showers."

Dad was thrilled when the lessons concluded. It was still questionable whether he gained pleasure in swimming but he had become acceptably proficient in the most basic swimming skills. So Mom "allowed" him to continue the fishing expeditions as long as he wore his life jacket. He still caught fish though he never ate them. Possibly working in a cannery had ruined his taste for fish.

The result of Dad's swimming lessons was not mastering the breaststroke or back stroke or learning to enjoy the water but a humorous book he wrote called "Chicken in the Pool." He had roughly sketched out stick figures to illustrate the coordinating words. On the cover he wanted to have a figure with floating devices on his arms dreaming of being a lifeguard. The book remained in his longhand, never printed.

For the rest of his life I never recall Dad venturing in to the bay, ocean, or swimming in a pool for sheer enjoyment. His skills in the water remained minimal, but his humor merited a gold medal.

21

Are We There Yet?

Imitating a Hollywood director shouting "A-C-T-I-O-N," Dad gestured with his free hand and in a commanding voice ordered "Okay, get closer together. Everybody look this way. Smile. Wave." Imitating actors taking the stage for an Oscar worthy performance, we gathered together, shoulder to shoulder. Dad focused his eight millimeter camera in our direction to record the moment, as he did on every single vacation. In reality we were mimes, showing facial expressions without words, doing our best to get the point across with gestures alone. Our hands flapped up and down as if there were invisible marionette strings attached, forcing us to make the motion of waving. Unfortunately, without capacity for sound, each reel of film was the image of the other. The only thing that distinguished which national park or tourist site we had visited was the handwritten title on the film's reel case.

Occasionally Mom would pipe up, "C'mon Sol. You get in the picture this time. I'll take it." She would change places with Dad, take hold of the camera, and we would, again, wave and smile. In theatrical style Dad would vary the script and gestures; pointing to the mountain behind us or motioning like he was diving into the lake in front of us. This was repeated throughout my childhood. These were summer vacations.

Vacations meant road trips, sometimes being the four of us and other years Nanny and Morris Daddy would join us. Our station wagon was equipped with a state-of-the-art feature in the late 1950s; a third seat that faced the rear. This feature wasn't popular for long-probably because the view was of the road just traveled as opposed to where we were headed. Judy and I thought the rear facing seat was "neat-o" and spent most of our travel days motioning and waving to the riders in the car behind us.

Breakfast, when the four of us traveled, was served in our own private "dining car." Mom and Dad stopped at a grocery store and purchased a variety package of single serving cereal boxes. Serrated marks showed where to punch out the small window enabling milk to be poured in. We pulled in to a rest stop as Mom unpacked the cereal. "Who wants Cheerios? Who wants the Corn Flakes?" Once finished with our satisfying meal, the plastic spoons and soggy boxes would be disposed of and we would merge back onto the road.

I loved it when Nanny came with us. She was the designated playmate for me. "Let's play the license game. How about 20 questions? Can you guess what's in my hand?" I could always rely on Nanny to join me in every single game. Along the way Judy and I took turns complaining. "Are we almost there? I'm hot. Roll down the window. She's crowding me. Tell her to move over. Nobody wants to play with me. I'm starved."

Finally two rules were put in place. Number one. We would finish our travel day at a roadside motel that had a swimming pool. After a few hours riding backwards or playing "I see an Oklahoma license on that blue car!" we all needed a break, mostly from each other and the confines of the car. It made no difference whether the water in the pool was algae green or crystal blue. We would stop early enough in the day so we could take a swim.

Dad would pull the car into the loading space in front of the reception area of a basic motel and park. We would wait for Mom to return with room keys, then run to open the door and flop on the bed in the air-conditioned room, leaving Dad at the car taking luggage off the roof. "C'mon girls. Help take stuff in." Dad's voice had an edge of annoyance to it along with exhaustion. "Fair is fair." This was his everyday response to our bickering.

Rule number two was put in place when my grandparents traveled with us. Morris Daddy occasionally grumbled about being too cold or too hot or uncomfortable on the long drive. Nanny would pipe up, "Oh Morris, stop complaining." So it was determined that whoever complained during the ride, excluding Judy and me, had to pay for the next restaurant meal. With a slight giggle Morris Daddy would intentionally object to conditions we encountered: the weather, the motel, the sightseeing. Then he would pick up the check anticipating, that according to the rule, there would be no resistance from Dad.

"Let's go to Sacramento," Mom suggested when discussing one summer vacation. "We can visit my cousins and see the California State Capital. The girls are a perfect age to visit the capital building." Off we drove to northern California. Mom's cousin, Ruth, her husband Stanley, their son and twin daughters, invited us to dinner at their home on the Sacramento River. Following the backyard barbecue, their son, Louie, serenaded us on the accordion. Louie was a tall, lanky, awkward thirteen year old. Though the songs he played soon escaped my memory, the squeeze box made an indelible impression. As Louie entertained us that warm summer evening the chords resonated as the air flowed around the bellows. I was enchanted. *I loved that sound. I wanted to learn to do that. I wanted to play the accordion*

All the way home I pleaded. "I just love the way the accordion sounds. Please, can I take lessons?" Once back home Mom drove me to the music store, rented an oversized instrument, then signed me up for beginning accordion lessons. Though I could hardly hold the ungainly device or see over the top, I happily attended classes for months attempting to sound like my cousin Louie.

The series of lessons culminated in a class recital. I was prepared to play "Lady of Spain." This was my first and last recital, my swan song. This confirmed to Mom and Dad that I had little musical talent. Now they had to devise a way, without hurting my pride, to get me to quit the accordion. It was close to my eleventh birthday and about that time we were required to renew the rental agreement or buy the squeeze box.

What I really wanted, besides the accordion, was a puppy since we had lost Trudy, our Dachshund, years earlier. It was a stroke of calculated genius when Mom and Dad offered me a choice for my birthday. "You can either get an accordion or a dog. You decide. What do you want most for your birthday?" They knew the answer.

My wish for a puppy was granted with the help of Nanny and Morris Daddy who contributed most of the $500 extraordinary expense for a white toy poodle. According to dollartimes.com today's buying power of $500 would equal a ridiculous amount of over $4000. We named the puppy after the popular Hungarian actress of the day, Zsa Zsa Gabor.

Though Zsa Zsa was my gift, when my spry small pet reached old age I left for college. Mom and Dad became the caregivers to Zsa Zsa who lived to the overripe age of nineteen. They got more than they bargained for when they gave a cute puppy to an excited eleven year old with no musical ability. But there is no doubt that, all in all, it proved to be desirable trade-off.

Each summer our road trip took us a little farther east. Gray mountains, blue skies, and lush green landscape of the Rocky Mountains greeted us on a trip to Colorado. We were advised by friends not to miss Estes Park, a resort area 7,500 feet above sea level. It was the middle of summer on the day we visited. But there was still snow on the sides of the road and the air was more than brisk. To San Diegans used to mild weather, it was freezing. We were unprepared in pedal pushers and short sleeve shirts. We drove through the wonderland huddled in the car with the heater blasting and luggage containing jackets safely packed on the roof of the car.

At one point Dad stopped the car at a rest area. "I have to go to the bathroom. I'll be right back." He tucked his head as far down as possible and ran towards the small stone building with a sign "Men" posted on the side. More than five minutes later, just as we began to wonder where he was, he jogged out of the restroom with his hands strategically placed in front of him. "My zipper broke. It's kaput" Dad chuckled. Our luggage was basically inaccessible. We stopped one more time on the way down the mountain to get lunch. Dad strategically kept his hands in front of him when we entered the restaurant. He then borrowed a napkin on the way out to cover the unexpected chill in an unexpected place.

In 1958 Morris Daddy and Nanny invited us to join them on a trip we could only have imagined in our dreams; the tropical Hawaiian Islands by way of a large ocean liner.

With exhilaration we boarded the SS Leilani in Long Beach, California. The ship's life was brief for the Leilani only cruised to

Nanny & Morris Daddy at the Captain's Dinner, on the Leilani to Hawaii

the islands from 1957 to 1959, when its parent company went bankrupt. We were used to breakfast out of cardboard boxes, so the floating hotel was the epitome of luxury.

For five days on the ship we walked the deck, enthralled by the white caps that rolled at the top of the ocean swells as far as the eye could see. The ship was more than a mode of transportation. Our days were filled with activities: dress up contests, hula classes, pool games, bingo, lei-making, and more food than we could consume. On the sixth morning at sea, the silhouette of Diamond Head came into view as we pulled into dock.

We disembarked to the sight of bare chested brown men in grass skirts and lovely long dark-haired women with necklaces of plumeria leis. They gracefully rolled their hips in time with ukulele music playing *"Oh, we're going to a hukilau, a huki-huki-huki-huki hukilau. Everybody loves a hukilau."* Morris Daddy chuckled during the show "I think they have a motor under their skirts." Dancers draped us with flowers as we gathered our luggage and set off to find a taxicab. We had reserved rooms at The Breakers Hotel at the cost of $12 per night. Hawaii was exotic, tropical, truly a primitive paradise the year before it was declared the 50th state in the union. This trip beyond the border of mainland America exceeded the dreams and imagination of a 12 year old who was coming of age.

22

What Happens in Vegas

"Whadoyasay we go to Las Vegas this weekend?" Dad rhetorically asked out of nowhere. Dad and Mom both loved Las Vegas. Though they were nickel and dime gamblers, they eagerly partook of the glitzy entertainment that had made Las Vegas famous. The city had gained a reputation for exciting and exotic shows, unveiling the first Follies, complete with topless dancers, in 1957. The "Strip" was without a doubt like no other place we had ever visited. It was loud, wild, and crowded. Mixed in with extravagant jubilees featuring scantily clad women were big name entertainers who headlined showrooms.

Las Vegas was the dream development in 1946 of a mobster named Bugsy Siegel. Siegel opened up the Flamingo Hotel with backing from the mafia and drug money. The city generated a level of excitement unequaled even in Hollywood. The real draw was money. Gambling was legal in Nevada so that plus extraordinary round-the-clock activities were a huge draw.

Our weekend adventure began with a five hour drive from San Diego. We arrived at the Sahara Hotel mid-afternoon. The legendary Sahara Hotel and Casino was the reputed hangout of Hollywood celebrity friends known as the "Rat Pack." The Rat Pack included Frank Sinatra, Dean Martin, Sammy Davis Jr., and Peter Lawford. They would often perform in groups at the Sahara or one of the other large hotel showrooms.

Judy and I, well below the legal gambling age of 21, were not allowed on the casino floor. We were just excited to be in the vicinity of the action, inching our way on the jewel tone carpet that edged the rows of slot machines and blackjack tables. The gigantic hotels and the bright lights created a circus like atmosphere. We stood behind the stanchions dividing the gambling area from the walkway. Mom and Dad wandered over to the slot machines and dropped nickels in, pulling the machine handle between each coin, then watching the machine respond. The spinning reels *whir-r-r-red,* then slowed to a stop. *Boing-boing-boing. If the pictures lined up, we would hear a scream "y-e-a-h, y-e-a-h!"* Then almost immediately lights would flash, a shrill siren sounded followed by the jingle of money dropping into the coin tray. Someone, hopefully Mom or Dad, had hit a jackpot!

Though Las Vegas geared entertainment towards adults, we enjoyed our own Vegas nights. On a typical evening Mom and Dad took us to dinner at the hotel coffee shop. After dinner we would find a convenience store on the strip,  each choose a teen magazine and our favorite candy bar. Back at the hotel Mom and Dad would escort us up the elevator to our room with instructions. "Don't open the door to anyone. Don't leave the room. We will come back and check on you. Have fun." We were ecstatic. We felt so grown-up. It was our Vegas too.

Reno, Nevada, was another gambling mecca. One memorable trip was destined to be cut short. We were younger on this trip so Mom and Dad had hired a babysitter to watch us at our motel one evening. The babysitter spent the entire evening braiding my long dark hair. By the time Mom and Dad returned I had a head full cornrows.

It had not been a winning night for Dad. The money allotted for our vacation was almost gone. It was questionable whether there was enough cash to get us home and credit cards were still a thing of the future. "I think we'll go home a day early," Dad casually mentioned.

The next afternoon Dad took a walk by himself. "I'll be back in a little bit," he mentioned as he left the three of us at the motel. A couple of hours passed and evening was approaching. Mom was getting worried when Dad didn't return. He finally arrived and had that sparkle in his eye. "Well girls, no need to hurry home. We don't need to pack up yet. I was lucky. I had a winning streak and won seven jackpots. Now we can stay an extra day." It didn't make sense to waste time worrying about Dad's ability to land on his feet.

23

The Happiest Place on Earth

"Just walk right on through like you know what you're doing. Don't stop." Dad said in an untypically low soft voice. "Go on ahead."

It was 1956, one year after the opening of "The Happiest Place On Earth."

Disneyland, the vision of Walt Disney, was located an hour and a half drive north in Anaheim, California. Disneyland had made front page headlines in newspapers throughout the country. The paper stated that 50,000 excited children and adults rushed the gates on opening day, July 17, 1955. The unlikely star and official mascot of the amusement park was a cartoon character; a mouse created by the Walt Disney Studio in 1928. This lovable mouse named Mickey greeted all who entered the hundred-and sixty-acre park. The same year the Mickey Mouse Club debuted on black and white television to great fanfare. In the words of Walt Disney "Who says we have to grow up? Laughter is timeless. Imagination has no age, and dreams are forever." This was promoted to be an attraction like no other in the world.

I was ten years old when Dad began our dinner table conversation over Porcupine Meatballs. These were an American comfort food made from ground beef mixed with rice cooked in tomato sauce, and were Dad's favorite. "I think it's time to see what Disneyland is like. How about it? Mom and I think it would be really fun." Judy and I bounced up from the table, our eyes wide as saucers. "When? Can we go Saturday?" "Yep. I think they've worked out all the bugs by now. So let's go see for ourselves," Dad chuckled.

I hardly slept the night before our adventure. My imagination ran wild. It was dream worthy. I had heard all about Sleeping Beauty's Castle, the Mad Tea Cups that swirled in dizzying circles, a Jungle Boat ride, and the special race cars that had recently been headlined in the news. I was dressed and ready early the following Saturday. We piled into our 1955 coral and white Oldsmobile sedan and headed to the Magic Kingdom. "Are we almost there? Are we almost there?" We were eager to see if "The Happiest Place on Earth" would live up to the hype in the newspaper and the advertisements heard on our TV console over the last year. We were expecting that Disneyland encompassed the fantasy of yesteryear, the latest trends of the present, and technology of the future, all in one place.

Dad pulled into the parking lot and was directed to a space by a young man dressed in a collared shirt complete with an applique of Mickey Mouse on the pocket. He pointed to the sign at the end of the row. Dad took a mental note of our location. "Remember we're parking in the Donald Duck row, so we can find our car at the end of the day."

Judy and I raced towards the ticket booth. "Hurry, c'mon. Let's get our tickets." Dad paid the $2.00 for each child's ticket book and $3.00 for each adult ticket book. Buying the booklet of ten tickets was more economical than paying for each ride separately. Each book contained tickets labeled A, B, C, D. The three "A" tickets were worth ten cents each, the rides being deemed less popular than the B, C, or D tickets. The three "D" tickets were valued at thirty-five cents each and were required for entrance to the best attractions such as the Jungle Boat.

Judy and I headed towards the gate with our tickets, Mom and Dad following behind. Above the entrance we could glimpse the Queen Anne style Main Street train depot where the Santa Fe and Disneyland Railroad circled the entire Magic Kingdom. "Wow, take a look at Mickey Mouse's face in flowers" I shrieked, unable to contain my enthusiasm at the sight of the bright flowerbed that adorned the entrance. With a cheery greeting "Welcome to the Magic Kingdom," the ticket taker punched a hole in each booklet.

As we entered Main Street, we were transplanted to the early 1900's and the nostalgia of days gone by. The street was filled with the harmony of a barbershop quartet, the smell of fresh popped corn, and the *clop-clop-clop* of horse drawn carriages. The red and white striped awning of the Carnation ice cream shop came into view. We made a note to come back later. But we were on a mission.

A well-publicized attraction at the time was the Junior Autopia cars. These required a valuable "D" ticket. The mini sized, brightly colored, convertible race cars allowed the driver to navigate over guide rails as the car went through a freeway replica complete with underpasses and bridges. The attraction represented the multi-lane highways of the future in the United States and the pint-sized vehicles could reach a rousing speed of about seven miles per hour for 4/10 of a mile.

Dad driving granddaughter Lindsay in Junior Autopia in 1978

At the end of Main Street we saw a sign directing us to Tomorrowland and then we saw the Autopia cars ahead.

The neon lights flashed on the sign displaying "Junior Autopia." The queue snaked back and forth making it impossible to tell how long it was. But it didn't matter as the anticipation of this attraction was enticing. According to the publicity, *This ride shouldn't be missed! If you don't do anything else, do drive the Junior Autopia.* We joined the end of the crawling line.

After more than an hour creeping back and forth, we could see the tracks, the shiny cars, and the point of entry. That's when Dad noticed the sign. ***You must reach this line ----------to drive the Junior Autopia cars.*** Dad realized I was too short to reach the 54" height requirement to drive. Knowing how disappointed I would be, Dad came up with a plan. "Don't stop in front of the sign. Just walk on through," he whispered. I glanced again at the sign. It was then I realized I was headed for a devastating letdown. "I'll give the attendant the tickets. You just walk on in," Dad continued.

It was our turn. I avoided looking up at the teenage ticket-taker in the race car uniform. Tears formed in the corners of my eyes. "Hi there. I want to get that sharp red race car" Dad schmoozed. "I won't go too fast cause I don't want to get a ticket." Dad handed the smiling teenager our "D" tickets. Slinking ahead, I continued to walk towards the red mini-car. Expecting that the ruse would be discovered, I quickly stepped into the car, slid over to the driver's seat, clicked the seat belt across my lap, and looked straight ahead as Dad scooted in beside me.

When all the cars were loaded with drivers and the attendant gave the signal to GO, I gently stepped on the gas and inched forward. Our red convertible crawled along the tracked roadway as the other autos stacked up behind me. It was my first time driving and I was a bit wary. Dad encouraged me "Baby, step on the gas. Push on the pedal." Slowly I accelerated to maximum speed. Though too short to drive by Disneyland requirements, I felt ten feet tall. I knew at that moment the real "Magic" at the kingdom was my very own dad.

Similar ploys worked throughout Dad's 93+ years. One Saturday afternoon in 2011, Mom, Dad, and I took an afternoon ride. Dad suggested we visit Cabrillo National Monument located a mile from their house. To access the grounds, there was an annual pass that cost $35 or a $15 fee for a single visit. A young man was stationed at the entry booth to allow those with proper credentials or tickets to enter. With the window closed, I slowed down, ready to stop. Then Dad, beside me in the passenger seat, pulled his library card out of his wallet and flashed it to the attendant. The guard smiled and waved us through the gate. Did Dad actually have an annual pass? I never knew and never asked.

I did know that Dad had "chutzpah" and who knew what he could accomplish armed with his gift of gab and his library card.

24

"Mah nishtanah...Why is this night different..."

Our family celebrated the commercial side of Christian holidays which most likely confused our non-Jewish friends and neighbors. We attached no religious significance to these days and joyfully decorated for the holiday of the month, whichever ethnic, religious, or national group made claim to it. From Easter eggs to matzo, from witches to menorahs, from Santa to shamrocks, we participated with enthusiasm.

Passover was an especially important Jewish holiday when we gathered with extended family and friends for a Seder, the ritual service celebrating the liberation of the Israelites from slavery in Egypt. For the eight days of the holiday bread products and flour was replaced with matzo, the flat unleavened bread that resembled a cracker. Corn and grains were also forbidden for Ashkenazi (Eastern European) Jews. Dad adhered to these traditions faithfully. Then when the sun finally set on the eighth day of Passover, Dad broke open the chocolate See's candy eggs made with corn syrup that had been saved from Easter baskets.

Mom, the girl from Idaho, most likely contributed to Dad breaking the kosher tradition of his childhood. On a date to the Carnation Restaurant on El Cajon Boulevard during college, Dad ate his first non-kosher hamburger and topped it off with a milkshake.

But at his core, Dad's Orthodox upbringing remained important to him throughout his life. He faithfully put on phylacteries, also known as tefillin. The purpose of tefillin is to remind the wearer of God's laws. These small black leather boxes contain scrolls of parchment with verses of the Torah. Leather straps are wrapped around the arm connecting the head, heart, and hand during morning prayers.

We watched Dad each day, except on Saturday (the Jewish Sabbath), in his bedroom, his back to the door, facing his open closet. He wore a beige wool newsboy cap on his head as he wrapped his arms with leather straps. His prayer book was placed open on the shelf over his sock drawer as he uttered his daily prayers in a respectful low voice. It seemed so spiritual, though all was done in a rote manner. While going through the motions directed in the most revered book in Judaism, he was concurrently reading the sports section of the San Diego Union newspaper. I choose to believe that God appreciated that Dad was a master at multitasking.

25

The Most Wonderful Time Of The Year

An intriguing opportunity was presented to Dad by a business associate. Alvin Strep was the owner of Teller's, a large discount department store located on University Avenue in the Hillcrest area of San Diego. Al asked Dad to partner with him and manage sales of fresh cut Christmas trees on the empty lot adjacent to the store. Though Dad had no experience or knowledge of the Christmas tree business, he set about researching it. He contacted the owners of a tree farm in Shelton, Washington, a city 30 miles from Tacoma. He got right to the point. "I am interested in going in the Christmas tree business. Can you tell an inexperienced Jewish kid about the trees? What kind do you have? What's the difference? Isn't a Christmas tree a Christmas tree? Yes, everything! Tell me everything I need to know to sell them." After deliberating, he could "see the trees for the forest." Little did Dad anticipate how the Christmas season would take over his life.

The tree frenzy began a week before Thanksgiving. Dad recruited a crew of off-duty firemen to sweep the vacant lot clean. They fenced the area, set up light poles, and lined up tables to create a checkout area. When the dirty work was completed, a temporary phone line was added along with a cash register and a small storage closet for basic carpentry equipment. Each day the excitement escalated and by midweek all that was missing were the trees themselves.

On Thanksgiving Day most American families were consuming an extraordinary amount of food commemorating Indians and Pilgrims feasting together in 1621. Dad sat at the head of the dining table on Thanksgiving evening with a plate full of turkey and marshmallow covered sweet potatoes surrounded by family and friends. But his mind was elsewhere.

The following day a semi-truck arrived at the empty primed tree enclosure and the rear door of the vehicle lifted. Dad and his workers focused on the fresh cut trees that were stacked up to the roof of the truck. Needles fell from the truck, prickly to the touch, and gold colored sap stuck to the gloved fingers of the men unloading the trees as they tossed them on the ground. An aroma described as strong, minty, clean, and earthy, collided in nostrils that had become lined with dust and dirt. All senses were awakened; as if the forest had come to the city.

For the next month Dad toiled from the crack of dawn until the moon was high in the sky. His scent would penetrate the night air creating an aura around him when he arrived home, swinging open the back door around ten o'clock. Pine needles would leave a Hansel and Gretel trail from the garage to the family room. Dad was in his uniform; a dirty winter jacket and old pants covered in gummy sap, and his brown boots blanketed with debris and dirt. On his head was an old hat pulled down to his eyebrows. While his eyes drooped with weariness, his smile was broad, puffing out his chilled red cheeks as if he were a chipmunk storing food.

Full of anticipation, we went to greet Dad, grabbing at the white canvas bags full of coins he gripped in his arms. The bags were heavy and we used both hands to carry each one. It was our job, our contribution in helping the family business, to count the dimes, nickels, and quarters taken in each day at the lot register. We considered our job vital and we took it seriously. We separated the coins into piles, then filled the paper coin rolls. Dad finished the job by counting the rolls, then tallying each on the deposit slip. Then he put his worn, dirty, wool jacket back on, gathered the bags, and left the house to make the nightly bank deposit.

This single lot became a cornerstone for the seasonal business. He humbly considered himself "The King of Christmas Trees," since at the time he was the largest supplier of live Christmas trees in San Diego. Innovative ads blared from radios throughout the day. *To-o-o-o-t, t-o-o-o-t...chug-a, chug-a, chug-a (the sound of a locomotive in the background).* *"Tellers trees are back again, Teller's Trees are back again." Chug-a chug-a, chug-a. "Last year we sold over 40,000 fresh Christmas trees. No tree over $2.88, up to 10 feet tall. Teller's Trees are back again"....T-o-o-o-t, t-o-o-o-t.*

Dad's goal was to cover all costs by the weekend closest to December 15th. This was the breakeven point, when he would negotiate to buy more trees for the final week before the holiday. The farms needed to unload the cut trees the week before Christmas when transactions were made to the benefit of both parties. Dad savored this time.

Judy and I pleaded "Puh-leze, puh-leze, can we go with you to meet the train and see the trees, puh-leze Dad?" "Okay girls, let's go. There's always room for one more," his often stated sentiment. Well into the evening, and excited to be on what we considered a midnight adventure, we arrived at the station to meet the shipment of trees. This was also when we picked out a tree for our living room that we would cover with tinsel and ornaments. Dad was there to direct the transfer of fresh trees from the train to the truck.

Whether there were still buyers late in the season was a risk, and created a stressful but exciting adrenaline rush that Dad thrived on. The week before Christmas was the culmination that determined whether the business would make a profit for the season.

For years the Christmas tree business grew. Dad leased more lots all around the city to sell the trees. In due time the six weeks of hard word provided an income that supported our family through most of the year. Dad hired his sister, Ida, and many of his friend's children to work the lots. Winter break was a good time to earn spending money for students.

One of the best workers was Stuart, a cocky college friend of Judy's from Los Angeles who attended San Diego State College. On a night when Stuart was managing a lot, a burly customer ambled around the grounds for close to an hour. He picked up tree after tree, studying the branches, height, and balance, hesitating at each as if he were purchasing something of far greater value than a Christmas tree. He finally chose his prize, a stately seven foot Douglas fir with branches that would support shiny glass ornaments and strands of lights. With both hands he lifted the tree and entered the checkout line. Stuart made small talk, "Hey, you picked a great tree, sir. Okay, that will be $2.88 plus twelve cents tax." He faced the register and punched in the numbers: 2-8-8 + 1-2. "If you would like a stand it will be twenty-five cents." "W-h-a-a-t?" the red-faced customer shouted, "Twenty five cents for the stand? You Jews are all alike."

That was all Stuart needed to hear. He grabbed the tree. "Sorry, this tree is not for sale." The loud mouth was stunned "Whadoyamean?" Without skipping a beat, the couple next in line piped up "We'll take that tree and we want a stand for it." The offender grabbed his wife by the arm and stormed out "Who do they think they are? We'll go someplace else" he growled. Without hesitation Stuart rang up $3.25, called over a worker to nail the wooden stand to the bottom of the tree, and smiled "Thank you and Merry Christmas to you." "H-m-m-m, good job kid," Dad responded when he heard the story.

By Christmas day Dad had cleared and cleaned all the lots. He had disposed of any leftover trees. Fences, wiring, and lights were removed; lots restored to their original condition. Exhaustion was forgotten. While others celebrated with holiday eggnog, Dad celebrated the season by knowing a job had been well done and he had made enough money to support the family until his next business opportunity came along.

Dad continued for years operating the tree business that had grown to eight lots. After we were both married, Judy and I managed one lot and sons-in-law, Ed and Chuck, managed another lot. One day my husband, Chuck, answered the phone on the lot "Schultz' Christmas Trees." There was silence. Then a loud voice bellowed "Jesus Christ! I paid a fortune to be known as Teller's Trees. Nobody knows Schultz' Trees."

Chuck immediately answered, "You need a better training program!"

Time and circumstances changed so Dad was forced to face the inevitable. Discount stores, grocery stores, and even pharmacies started to offer fresh Christmas trees for sale. The tree business had been profitable for many years and had run its course. For Dad it was a season of passion, risk, hard work, excitement, and success. From beginning to end the tree business was his Advent calendar, the countdown to Christmas. He loved every minute of it and so did we.

We weren't cognizant how unique our celebrations were when Chanukah overlapped with Christmas. We lit the Chanukah candles each of eight nights with a blessing, ate latkes, played the dreidel game, and exchanged gifts, all in the midst of shiny ornaments hanging from a fir tree.

26

Learning to Drive

The weeks before my 16th birthday were filled with anticipation - and anxiety. Being one of the youngest in my junior class in high school, I was also one of the last of my classmates to come of age-sweet 16. Being sixteen meant focusing on: boys, cars, and music. Sixteen is the legal age in California to marry with consent, consent to sexual activity with someone aged 16 and over, and drink beer or wine with a meal if accompanied by someone over 18.

I was not concerned about getting married or drinking alcohol at that crossroad in my life. It was qualifying to legally drive a vehicle that put my nerves on edge. The law stated that to receive a license a potential driver had to pass Driver's Education class and successfully pass a written exam and physical driving test. The most dreaded obstacle was the requisite "behind-the-wheel" test, maneuvering a car on city streets in the presence of a DMV driving examiner.

February 25th was my 16th birthday and Mom had written an excuse for me to skip school. The hurdle between being chauffeured and driving myself was the obstacle I wanted to navigate. Mom, Dad, and I headed to the Department of Motor Vehicles so I could take the feared exam.

Judy had passed all the requirements two years prior

earning a California Driver's License. Dad could hardly contain his excitement about the gift Mom and he bought her as a high school graduation gift. The fireball orange Ford had been discreetly hidden in the garage of Lois and Walter, old family friends. Following graduation ceremonies Mom began, "Let's stop by the Morings for a few minutes. Lois invited us over for ice cream and cake to celebrate your graduation, Judy." After congratulatory hugs, Lois casually asked, "Judy, could you please go in the garage and get the ice cream out of the freezer?" We crept up behind her in anxious anticipation as she opened the door to the garage. We waited for a shriek of joy, an overwhelming gasp of utter pleasure. Not sure what she was seeing, Judy was speechless. Her bright blue eyes opened wide and her jaw dropped to the floor.

Parked in the garage was a car unlike any other. Dad had purchased this lowered bright orange vehicle with shiny chrome hubcaps from a man who had taken it away from his teenage son.

Judy & her friend in 1961 with her high school graduation gift

A brilliant wax job made the color shine like a lighted pumpkin on Halloween night. The Ford was the perfect vehicle to compete on a racetrack or in a car show. "Whaddaya think?" Dad gleamed. "Is this a great car? You're gonna be the talk around school. Let's give it a try!" Dad shouted. He burst with pride as Judy stood in shock. We all jumped in for a ride around the block, Judy in the driver's seat. Dad rolled down his window as Judy turned the key ninety degrees in the ignition. The Ford purred to action as the gear was shifted to reverse, and we backed down the driveway. The car vibrated and *v-v-room* we were off, traveling through the quiet neighborhood like a tsunami overtaking the coastline. Judy drove a few blocks, her eyes barely peeking over the steering wheel in the flashy, ostentatious cop magnet. In a short time the horn honked with every right turn. A persistent electrical problem could never be properly fixed and once smoke started coming out from under the driver's seat, it was time to let it go.

Judy preferred to drive the other car, the Morris Minor. This small British made car was unobtrusive but also had a manual four speed transmission. It did not deter her. She learned to depress the clutch and shift gears, of which she was mildly competent, and I was grateful when she chauffeured me to school dances. The radio would be blaring a top ten tune, such as Paul Anka's "Lonely Boy" or "Venus" sung by heartthrob, Frankie Avalon. We would jerk down the street every time she shifted gears, our Morris Minor bouncing to the beat of the music.

Now it was finally my turn. We arrived at the DMV, signed in, then sat in the plastic chairs waiting for my name to be called. Finally, "Miss Schultz" a serious middle-aged man called out, "Please follow me to your vehicle." With a clipboard in hand, he narrowed his eyes, making no attempt to ease my nerves.

I gingerly climbed in the driver's side of the Oldsmobile. I felt comfortable in our car. I had practiced with Dad in various parking lots in the neighborhood multiple times. The lever on the side of my seat had been released and the seat adjusted as far forward as possible so I could reach the gas pedal and brake. The top of my head was still below the seat headrest and I was aware that the car appeared to drive itself when viewed from behind. I was well versed in street signs, in coming to a complete stop at STOP signs, and how to stop then cautiously turn right on a red light that was within the law of California. I had practiced how to accelerate when merging lanes; how to look in the rear view mirror AND over my shoulder when changing lanes to check the blind spots.

The portly man in the tweed sport jacket opened the passenger's door and slid into the seat. His appearance was unsettling. He sat stone-faced next to me, raising his eyebrows and muttering under his breath. We settled in. He asked me a few questions and marked his clipboard. "Name?" "Birth date?" His face had no expression and there was no acknowledgment that this was my birthday. I could feel my heart pounding. My palms were wet and sweat began to build from my armpits under my collared blouse. I bit the inside of my cheek-a nervous habit. "You can start the car, Miss Schultz." I heard his voice but it didn't register in my brain. "Okay, Miss Schultz, you may proceed" he repeated. In a tense and nervous state of mind, I tried to focus on the task at hand. He repeated for the third time, "You may start the car, Miss Schultz."

I cautiously turned the key in the ignition. I released the brake and eased forward with my foot on the gas. "Turn right out of the parking lot, then make another right at the corner," the examiner's monotone voice filled the air. I looked both ways out of the parking lot, slowly releasing my foot off the brake then ever so slightly pressed on the gas pedal. I breathed a sigh of relief. I was off to a good start. I turned right, then at the corner carefully looked both ways before making another right. "Young lady, see those orange cones? Pull up and park between those two cones."

Up to this point I had felt prepared. Up to this point I was somewhat confident in my skills to drive, NOT to park. I was not great at any kind of parking and parallel parking was particularly difficult for me. Nonetheless, I pulled forward slowly. Digging deep in my brain to remember the rules of the parallel parking, I pulled up in front of the first cone, backed up about half way and turned the wheel clockwise to get close to the curb. All was going well until I heard a muted *thump*. I had bumped into the back cone. It was as if the examiner had discovered a winning lottery ticket. "Oh, sorry, you hit the cone" he smirked. "Miss, you have not qualified for a license. You have failed the driving test. You need to practice and come back again." I was stunned. I could hardly see as my eyes clouded over with tears. I went forward and made one last right turn back into the parking lot. I got out of the car, trying nonchalantly to wipe away the tears rolling down my cheeks.

I entered the crowded noisy waiting room and gingerly walked over to break the news to Mom and Dad. "It was stupid," I stammered. "I didn't even get to show how good a driver I am," I whispered. Their smiles turned to looks of sympathy. Immediately Mom cheerfully piped in "Let's go eat lunch, and you'll feel better. Then maybe we can come back later. You can try again when you are more relaxed."

And that is what we did. I dried my tears of disappointment and overcame failure with a hamburger and fries. On a full stomach, I gained confidence. This time I knew what to expect. It was mid-afternoon when we trekked back to the DMV. When my name was called, I knew the routine. Seeking to control my nervousness, I looked straight ahead, walked to the parking lot, and got into the car. This was a fresh start. Though my passenger was a different examiner, I soon discovered the process and route was the same. I turned on the ignition, proceeded slowly, turned right out of the parking lot, turned right again, pulled up along side one of the orange cones, backed up slowly and bumped the back cone. I failed again!

For the next few months Dad and I practiced parallel parking diligently. Sometime during the year I worked up the gumption to take the driving test a third time. I did pass the exam on the third try though, to this day, I feel that parallel parking is an optional skill, not an important benchmark for excellent driving ability.

Dad didn't take any chances on a hot rod for me. I shared one of the family cars. This was most often a 1965 red Ford Mustang. Many years and a few cars later Mom and Dad "sold" me a yellow Ford Mustang for the sum of one dollar. The small note on a scratch paper read "1/16/71. This certifies I have given the Mustang 1967-7ROIC20137-6 to my daughter Susan Schultz Gold. Sol Schultz."

I should have kept that amazing gift.

27

The Unpopular War

The conflict in Vietnam began in 1954 after the rise to power of Ho Chi Minh and his communist Viet Minh party in North Vietnam. In 1960 the United States military had 900 personnel in South Vietnam. By 1962, under President Kennedy, U.S. military personnel had grown to 11,000.

Vietnam was as far away geographically as it was in my mind. I was a teen submerged in the every day drama of high school. In my world I was more interested in the Friday night football games than discussing daily headlines about war in a country most of us couldn't find on a map. I was out of touch with real news. But the war was escalating and student protests at colleges across the country were building.

At the end of my sophomore year I was concentrating on vying for one of four positions as a school songleader. I had no real knowledge of football or basketball, the games that we would be expected to cheer for. I was short on talent and could not complete any death-defying gymnastic moves. But I did excel in school spirit. The competition was heavy and I practiced tirelessly. Mom, always supportive, crafted a blue culotte and blue and white striped blouse for the school tryouts.

The morning the student body assembled Mom and Dad offered words of encouragement along with hugs before taking their seats in the wooden bleachers. "Just do your best and have fun. Remember to smile." That afternoon students gathered in the quad and my name was announced as one of the winners. I was ecstatic, feeling proud and somewhat cocky. I was on top of the world hurrying the three blocks home accompanied by a small group of friends. I could hardly wait to share the news with Mom. I pushed open the front door and the words tumbled out "Mom, Mom, guess what? I won. I made it. I'm gonna be a songleader next year." Mom met us with a broad smile and her eyes told me she was proud but her first words were not directed to me. She looked directly at my friends "Aren't you lucky? That's nice that you won but the nicest thing is that you have such wonderful friends to be here with you and share the news. What a lucky girl you are." She smiled and hugged each girl.

At that moment I didn't fully appreciate Mom's praise for my friends, rather than excitement for me. The significance of her actions stayed with me and years later I realized the important and valuable lesson she had taught me.

Point Loma High School
Songleader 1962

28

It's a Privilege

A 'dyed in the wool' Democrat, Morris Daddy was a Liberal through and through. He studied the candidates platforms and the issues and voted with his head and his heart. He followed the news religiously, read multiple newspapers, Time Magazine, and The New Yorker.

The New Yorker was full of essays, commentary, and criticism of current topics. The magazine's target audience was affluent, educated readers, and a great majority tended to be politically liberal. *The New Yorker* influenced the opinions of readers capable of having opinions in the first place. It was quoted that "It provides intellectual delight to those capable of intellectual pleasure."

Morris Daddy was challenged by the journal. One sunny day on his morning walk Morris Daddy was visibly upset when he opened the back door to our house. "My dear Charlotte," he began, with a frown on his forehead "I sometimes have to read an article in the New Yorker twice to understand it fully. I should be able to read the magazine one time and comprehend everything." Morris Daddy was of the rare breed who looked up the definitions of words he didn't know in Webster's dictionary. He was unusually inquisitive, curious, delving into understanding various policy and platforms of candidates running for elected offices. He considered his right to vote a privilege and the responsibility of being an American citizen.

Mom followed in his footsteps. She served as a political adviser to all of us when we were old enough to vote. We took her word as gospel, knowing she had taken the time to study the candidates and their platforms.

In June 1963 I graduated from Point Loma High School. It was time to venture out into the world. Was I ready?

High School Graduation: Dad, Mom, Me, Huki

29

Taking Flight

The handsome, young, charismatic president dazzled us with his head full of thick wavy hair. "As a nation, we have no deeper concern, no older commitment and no higher interest than a strong, sound and free system of education for all. In fulfilling this obligation to ourselves and our children, we provide for the future of our nation-and the future of freedom."

We were among the adoring crowd in June 1963 as President John F. Kennedy delivered a graduation address at San Diego State College. Thirty thousand admirers had traveled from near and far to put eyes and ears on the 35th President of the United States. The Kennedys portrayed youth and glamour. It was a new image of the presidency. They weren't much older than we were. The most powerful leader of the free world was speaking at the very campus where Mom and Dad met and where Judy was a flourishing student.

My sister had desperately wanted to go away to college. But Mom and Dad had an anthology of stories told by friends whose children had left San Diego to attend college. Partying had led them back home after failing their freshman year. "Look what happened to...She went to parties all the time and ended up flunking out." They insisted Judy spend two years at home before going away to school.

President Kennedy's speech coincided with my high school graduation. It was expected that I would go to college but, unlike my sister, I had no dreams of going away. High school days had been carefree and memorable. San Diego was home. I had no reason to leave. I was a seventeen year old with no direction, plans, or goals.

I took the ACT college entrance exam and mailed my one and only application to San Diego State College. It was a decision without thought, an easy road to higher education. SDSC was primarily a school for commuters in 1963. I expected college to be an extension of high school, basically Grade 13. I was confident that the transition to college would be easy and natural, only with more of everything: students, subject options, and activities.

I soon found out that I was unprepared for college. My freshman year was a shocking letdown. I felt overwhelmed, lost in the crowd of unfamiliar faces. I had made a conscious decision not to go through sorority rush. Who needed it? I knew 'everyone' in high school and many of my close friends were also going to State. I expected my existing circle of friends would only grow larger as I met new acquaintances in and between classes. The trappings of a sorority and 'suddenly sisters' wasn't really appealing.

But a few weeks after matriculating, it became obvious that naiveté had clouded my thinking. Most of my high school friends had, in fact, joined sororities. They were thrust into a sisterhood requiring time and commitment. Their sorority obligations became a priority. It wasn't that they snubbed me, but I was no longer part of their circle. I had been secure as part of a boatload of friends and was now drifting solo with nowhere to drop anchor.

The daily twenty-five minute commute to the campus was a drag. I went through the motions of campus life comprised of attending class lectures then walking through the quad in search of a familiar face. Among thousands of contemporaries, I was alone and lonely. My daily drive home was void of energy. I felt like an old flashlight battery; flickering for a few minutes when the switch is moved to ON, then quickly dying out.

Mid-freshman year my health deteriorated. An annoying sore throat, extensive fatigue, and a low grade fever hung on. What was first diagnosed as the flu ended up being confirmed as mononucleosis. It was commonly known as "the kissing disease" since it was spread through saliva. The ugly truth was that with minimal human connections on campus, I hadn't meaningfully interacted with anyone. The fact that I had contracted the "kissing disease" was a bad joke, like salt in a wound.

During that first year of college there were few things to brighten my day. I am embarrassed to acknowledge that lunch, even when eaten alone, was a highlight. This was especially true one day when I packed myself a delicious meal of leftover fried chicken from the previous night. In a hurry that Thursday, I grabbed my books, sweater, keys and (supposedly) my much anticipated cornflake crusted drumstick. Always cutting it close, I pushed past the 65 mph speed limit; my eyes darting between the rear view mirror and the road ahead fearing a black and white. I arrived at the sprawling campus, found a parking spot and, breathlessly, ran across campus. I eased into a rear seat in the classroom just as the professor greeted us "Hola estudientes" and continued to ramble in Spanish.

The lecture, totally in the language of our neighbors to the south, concluded a very long hour and a half later. I was eager for the break to savor my brown bag treat. I reached my hand under my metal desk probing for my lunch. With no success, I got out of the desk squatting to get a better look. *Okay, where is it? I am sure I put it under my desk. It's not there.*

H-m-m-m, maybe I left it in the car. I trekked back three blocks to the sea of cars in the massive parking lot. I searched the front and back seats, under and between the seats. No lunch. I was irate. *That's it. Someone in my class stole my lunch. I am sure it had been placed under the desk and someone had the NERVE to steal it right under my nose where I was sitting. I can't believe this place. I hate it here.* I muttered all the way to the cafeteria then purchased a bag of chips to partially satisfy my growling stomach.

What I didn't know was that Dad had found my lunch at home, right where I left it. His protective fatherly side sprung into action. He found my class schedule, drove a half hour to campus, parked the car, and headed to my classroom. He carefully opened the back door a sliver and heard the professor lecturing in Spanish. His eyes took in the scene until he caught sight of the back of my head. He was in the right place. He casually poked his arm in the doorway handing the brown paper bag to an inattentive male sitting within arm's reach. "P-s-s-s-t" he pointed to me and whispered, "Can you give this to that girl in the red dress?" He handed over the bag.... and that is where it rested....and was surely consumed by the appreciative student.

I arrived home that evening still annoyed. "Can you believe it? Someone stole my lunch today, right from under my desk in my Spanish class!" The silence at the dinner table was deafening. Then Dad, in a shocked voice piped up "Te-r-r-r-ible. That's absolutely terrible! Who would do something like that?" In truth he had confessed his special delivery to Judy. She warned with an outcry, "Don't ever tell Suzi what you did. She'll be mortified. She'll never forgive you." I, truthfully, would have been embarrassed, but it was years before Dad could bring himself to divulge the lunch delivery. Someone had, indeed, taken my lunch.

When the second semester of school approached I was encouraged by Mom to go through sorority rush. Mom hoped this would be helpful in meeting and making new friends. I would surely find a sense of belonging in a sorority. There was one Jewish sorority on campus. Judy was an active member and served as President during her years at SDSC. While this was an option, I really wanted to join a different house that many of my high school friends had pledged.

After attending many rush parties held by my preferred sorority, invitations for final preference were handed out. I was stunned when I did not receive one. Kappy, an old friend I had known for years, and a member of the house I desired, asked if I would meet her at a cafe. After a welcome hug, she hesitantly began to speak, "We really wanted to ask you to join the house but we can't. Our national chapter contacted us. We have a quota and we can't pledge any Jewish girls. I am so sorry." The rest of the conversation was a blur. I had never experienced anti-Semitism personally directed at me before. It was a poignant eye-opener that this was the world we lived in. The Jewish sorority welcomed me and I went through the gestures of being a good pledge, then active member. But this didn't help the emptiness I was feeling.

During the summer of 1964, Judy and I left home for a six week summer school session at UCLA in Los Angeles, two hours north of San Diego. We were looking forward to the experience of living in the dorms. The living quarters had a view of the imposing prestigious campus amid this town full of struggling actors and celebrities, close to the heart of the film industry. It was a taste of independence that we both needed. Students from all over the world provided a diversity we had not encountered during our childhood. The experience in the first week alone was exhilarating but was quickly shattered with sadness.

We received a sobering call from Mom. Our beloved Morris Daddy had suffered a fatal heart attack during his morning walk at the age of 84. We were in shock. From our perspective, with Morris Daddy's healthy lifestyle, he had seemed immortal. We returned home grief-stricken for the funeral. The week was spent reminiscing and providing comfort to each other. Nanny, her memory failing, repeatedly asked "Where's Morris?" After being told "He just went out for a walk," she was content. Then minutes later she would again ask "Where's Morris?"

A week later Judy and I compartmentalized our sadness and returned to summer school at UCLA. We had one more month to experience life living on campus before returning home to commute to San Diego State in the fall.

One evening, midway through my uneventful sophomore year at San Diego State College, I sat with Mom as she took her nightly bath. She loved to soak in the warm tub each night. If I had some news, some problem, or was seeking some advice, I would go into the bathroom for a therapy session while she bathed. The closed toilet seat served as my chair situated adjacent to the tub. It was an intimate time for me or any other family member to share our thoughts through the steam emitted by the hot water. Mom had all the answers, and the tub was where she relaxed. We chatted for a few minutes as I told her about my day. She looked up at me with sincere concern. "Dad and I have been thinking. College should be the best time of your life. You haven't been happy for the past two years and we're going to look at colleges and find a place for you to go that will make you happy."

Mom took the words of Khalil Gibran to heart-
If you love somebody, let them go.
For if they return, they were always yours.

30

Finding Happiness

In the months after Mom had encouraged me to leave the nest, we reviewed college catalogs. The University of Arizona peaked my interest. The campus in Tucson was just a six-hour drive from San Diego. The U of A offered a degree in fashion design and merchandising that sounded interesting. On the negative side, out of state tuition was expensive. The $800 per semester tuition was a far cry from the $45 tuition at SDSC per semester. When I received my acceptance letter, Mom and Dad were as eager for me to attend as I was.

The summer of 1965 flew by quickly. In August Mom helped me stuff my suitcases with my homemade culottes, madras shorts with matching tops, and Peter Pan collared blouses. We had fashioned these wardrobe pieces without any real knowledge of Arizona's co-ed fashions and trends. Dad carried my suitcases and bed linens to the car. I lugged my treasured sewing machine, placing it beside me in the back seat as the three of us began my journey towards independence.

The highway to Tucson from the Arizona border is straight with little of interest other than cactus and desert landscape. Dad kept within a few miles of the speed limit as we became aware of highway patrol cars stationed behind the desert shrubs. It was a quiet ride. We were buried in our thoughts, aware that

I was heading down a new path, finding my way, finally leaving the comforts of home.

We were thankful that air conditioning had recently become a popular amenity in the automobile industry. The heat sizzled on the car's hood as I rolled down the window to confirm the thermometer on the dashboard was working. It registered 105 degrees, approaching heatstroke range, and was only tolerable due to the lack of humidity. The dry heat eliminated that uncomfortable sticky feeling but it was hard to catch a breath when it felt like an oven door had been opened mid-baking. We stopped to fill up the car with gas and stepped outside to stretch our legs. Within a few minutes we felt parched, more like raisins than grapes.

Finally, 400 miles from San Diego, the stately buildings of the University of Arizona came into view. The U of A, founded in 1885, had stately brick structures surrounding "Old Main," a fountain centerpiece. The 20,000 student campus was almost double the student population at San Diego State College. Students ambled around Old Main: chatting, laughing, snacking. "Wow, take a look. I guess we were wrong about what the kids wear here." I observed the overwhelming number of students dressed in jeans, jean shorts, cowboy hats, and cowboy boots. "Let's go find your dorm," Mom cheerfully suggested.

We followed the written directions to Sonora, my assigned high-rise dorm. We began to unpack the car, lugging the bedding and suitcases to the elevator. I opened the door to my designated room finding two bunk beds divided by a closet on either side facing the beds. A desk with four cutout areas for chairs ran the length of the room. We continued carrying bags to my room, stacking my stuff on one of the desks and bunks. When all of my belongings had been placed in my new home, it was time for Mom and Dad to leave.

It had been a physically and emotionally exhausting day. Dad spoke up "How about dinner? All this work has made me hungry." We drove to the center of this bustling college town, then stopped at a cafe for our final meal together before Mom and Dad were to drive back to California. My anxiety

Off to the University of Arizona - 1965

was rising as Dad paid the bill. I realized I didn't know one person on campus. I was excited yet nervous and could already feel homesickness creeping in. This was a pivotal moment in my life and in theirs.

We pulled up to the dorm and Dad put the car in park. Students lingered around the entry, carrying their belongings, hugging family and laughing with friends. Dad stepped out of the car. He gave me hug "Okay baby, have fun. Write us soon." I felt my eyes well up with tears.

Mom stepped out of the car and leaned towards me.

She hugged me tightly then held me at arms distance. "Remember, when you get lonely, look at the moon. Know that I will be looking at the same moon each night and we will never be far apart." With that, they got back in the car and headed west towards the red glow of the sun as it dropped below the horizon. I watched the taillights get smaller until they were no longer visible. Timidly, but with determination, I turned towards the tall stucco building that would be my home for the next year. I was on my way.

The first letter from home was a salve for my loneliness. It was dated September 16, 1965, two weeks after I arrived at University of Arizona. I missed everything: my family, my dog, the comforts of home and the familiarity of San Diego.

Suzi Schultz -

This is your father writing! Well, I am so nice I am a little "nachious". I have not been a little "crenky" just good, good, good!

Went to Nelsons for Pot Luck tonight - lost $2 at poker! It is rainy, cold and not nearly so warm as Tucson! The dog enjoys the attention showered upon her but really-to stand at the shower and whine cause I won't let her in — well.

Enclosed is a picture of your old friend Herman the Hermit - a N.J.B. (nice Jewish boy).

Have to bed down now cause its 12:15 but love you real lots.

Love from Mom, Huk, and Old Yeller Daddy*

*Dad's nickname described his short fuse; anger displayed by a quick yell and, just as quick, a total lapse of memory of the explosion or cause of it. We were used to it and endeared him with the pseudonym 'Old Yeller.'

On the back side of this first letter was a note from Mom:

Hi Sweetie,

We got your letters today—It was so nice to hear from you. Doug sounds real nice. All of the rest of the boys do too.

I am on a very interesting case in the jury. A colored man is being charged with assaulting an officer. I have to go back tomorrow. I'll let you know how it comes out. I think the officer was prejudiced against the colored man. I love you very much and hope you are happy.

Love and Kisses, Mom

In a short time my nostalgia dissipated. The layers of my coddled shell peeled off like skin following a tingly sunburn.

I met new friends and adjusted to dorm life, finding my own path through the maze. Mom was right. College life was already in contention to be the best years of my life and I was only nineteen.

Arizona rapidly became the blood in my veins. Each season painted a different canvas. In spring a variety of wildflowers covered the desert floor; displaying a rainbow of colors against the dirt. The arms of the Saguaro cactus topped by blossoms reached up to the sky. The Sonora desert was alive with insects and spiny lizards, toads, and turtles. Fall brought a different tapestry of flora; bold yellow and purple wildflowers blanketed the sandy floor. Winter brought on the harshness of the gray-green spike covered cactus.

I had never experienced evenings in spring, fall, and early summer when the temperature coaxed many to sit outside on the roof of the dorm chatting with friends in shorts and sleeveless tops. A warm evening breeze provided respite from the scorching heat of the day. At night the sky turned coal black with a million twinkling stars appearing like fireflies.

Mom and Dad never discussed the financial burden of attending college out of state. Somehow they paid my tuition and expenses. My monthly allowance for incidentals was $50. Weekday meals were included in the dorm cafeteria, but weekend meals had to be covered by my allowance. I used my skills at sewing to offer simple alterations in the dorm and earn extra spending money.

Sunday morning long distance phone calls were my touchstone to home. We did our best to keep the expensive calls short. During the five minute conversations I rambled "I got a good grade on my Chemistry test but not so good on my Western Civ midterm. I went out with a cute boy the other night." I felt a sense of relief sharing the good and the bad news. Any unhappy news I shared remained foremost with

Mom and Dad until they heard a cheery voice from me the following Sunday.

The following letter was written the week before Parent's Weekend at University of Arizona.

October 16, 1965

Dear Suzi,

This is O.M.S. (Old Man Schultz) writing. My, you certainly have action going at A.U. I like the Shakespearean boy you are going out with — you know "Too-pay or not too-pay" that is the question.

We are going up to Rose Bowl to see State play LA State.

We are looking forward to seeing you next week and having a great time. Don't get me a date as I am going steady with Mama. This girl shows off her I.Q. sometimes. You know I think it was 2 x 72 not 144 as we were led to believe.

Well have to go watch TV football now. See you next week.

Love, Daddy and Group

Phone calls were interspersed between letters. Mom shared the news from home and Dad shared corny jokes. I wrote back, sharing news of classes, friends, and campus life. With each letter, the longing for San Diego was less pronounced. I no longer pined for home. I loved college life and Arizona.

Thursday.

Dearest Suzi:

Well - it's my turn to write to the Tucson Kid! We drew straws and I got the short one - you! Hee! Hee!

Glad you got good in Chem.

I have been rebuilding one of the apartments as a teenager tenant remodeled it a bit - he smashed the shower door - broke the toilet bowl & ran his fist thru the wall! -better his head through the wall!

Did you hear about the executive that got a dog for his wife - his friend wanted to know how he made the trade.

Little boy (looking at little girl) "Her neck's dirty." Other little boy "Her does?"

We are watching Dean Martin Show and it is real good. "Oh give me a home -Where the buffalo roam — and I'll show you a filthy place."

I'm going to L.A. tomorrow am on business and Saturday fishing - yea!

Yep! I'll take you when you come home.

Well peanut, guess this is all for now so will say good nite and we love you.

> *Old Daddy Shloyme*

I was excited to travel home for Christmas vacation in 1965, after five months away. Though I hadn't grown an inch in stature, my growth in confidence and independence had reached new heights. I felt self-assured, ready to fly on my own.

I wanted to spend the couple of weeks at home sharing my college experiences and enjoying family time. I hadn't seen my beloved grandmother, Nanny, for months-even before I left for Arizona. Mom had not wanted us to visit her in her confused and frail state. Nanny was bedridden and unable to verbally communicate. Mom wanted us to remember her as she was; full of kindness, compassion, and love. Nanny suffered from what was referred to in those days as 'hardening of the arteries' but most likely would be classified as Alzheimer's today.

Since before Morris Daddy's death the previous year we had noticed a rapid decline in her short-term memory and her increasing confusion. She would end every car ride with "Well, thanks for the buggy ride." Mom visited often and Nanny had round-the-clock care at her home until her dying day. On one hand it was a gift for us to remember Nanny as vibrant and so alive, but, in hindsight, we never got to say goodbye and express our love for this cherished woman.

On December 25, 1965, Mom received the feared call from Nanny's caretaker. "I'm afraid that Lottie has passed away." It was so typical of Nanny to wait until late at night on Christmas day so any festivities wouldn't be ruined.

For years Mom had resisted moving from our Curtis Street home. She wanted to be within walking distance of her parents and enjoyed Morris Daddy's daily visit. After Nanny's passing, Dad persuaded Mom to buy a home on a hill in the Fleetridge area of Point Loma. The area boasted large custom built California homes on curved streets. Mom was uncertain. She was very nervous about spending a 'fortune' on a home. The $50,000 list price seemed out of reach. "It's so expensive Sol. I don't think we can afford it." Dad was eager to move. "Don't worry Charlotte. We can make this work." Mom believed he could.

While I was hundreds of miles away at college, Mom and Dad moved three miles from the Curtis Street home they had built. Their new home was previously owned by a European couple. The master bathroom came equipped with an unexpected item; a bidet, common in Europe, but a new experience for Mom. The house on the hill at 3911 Point Loma Avenue became their final home.

31

He Found His Fit

The successful renovation of the Sumner Apartments gave Dad a boost of self-confidence. The year of backbreaking work had not worn him out but filled him with energy and hunger for more. It was his beginning in an industry that fed him the nourishment he had been looking for. Real Estate seemed to provide an appealing balance of risk and reward. With eagerness and enthusiasm he completed the required real estate classes and earned his license.

He jumped into the business wholeheartedly. It was a prime time for real estate in booming San Diego. Dad's California Real Estate License allowed him to represent both sides of a transaction. Opportunities in real property seemed endless and he was eager to explore them. In due time he bought vacant land, commercial buildings, multiple rental apartments, and land leases. Dad put together limited partnerships and successfully built a number of apartment units. He was in his element.

Dad built the Park Palms Motel with a group of investors (family and friends)

"Charlotte, I need you to sign these papers," Dad

said as he pointed to each signature line on official documents. After the first few transactions, Mom signed the documents Dad presented to her without question, no matter if he was buying or selling. Mom had stopped worrying. She had confidence that Dad's can-do attitude, combined with good business sense, would bring success. She didn't waste time stressing over what might happen, but told him emphatically "Sol, I don't care what you're buying or selling, what papers I have to sign, just as long as you give me my allowance on Monday." That was the arrangement that worked for them. He learned he could work whatever business deal he wanted. He just made sure when Monday morning arrived, so did his check made out to "Charlotte Schultz."

In 1960, Mission Valley became the heart and hub of San Diego. Located close to downtown, the beach and bay, it was prime for development. The Mission Valley Shopping Center opened in February of 1961 and a building boom followed. Investors came from all over and each one wanted a sliver of this delicious pie. In 1965, a $27 million bond was passed allowing construction to begin on San Diego Stadium with a capacity of over 50,000. The San Diego Chargers played the first football game ever at the stadium in August 1967.

With close to perfect weather San Diego had become a major tourist destination. Dad was fortunate to invest in and become a partner in the construction of one of the first motels located at the west end of Mission Valley. The Circle 7/11 Motel boasted close to 200 rooms and a restaurant known as Ricky's. The coffee shop quickly acquired a reputation for its breakfast Dutch Baby and World Famous Apple Pancakes. Dad settled into an office at the motel when he took on the position of General Manager in addition to being a partner. He spent his days circulating throughout the motel and restaurant. The Circle 7/11 Motel became Dad's second home.

He continued to invest in other projects for himself, family members, and friends, creating limited partnerships. Each successful venture fed into the next one. When he put the call out, "If you want in, I need xxxx thousand for this deal," no one bothered asking questions. They just simply wrote a check in the amount requested.

His integrity and honesty were above reproach. His measure of success was seeing a great return for all the partners. In her old age, one of the regular investors, then widowed, commented, "I wouldn't have anything if it weren't for our investments with Sol." His motto was, "Be fair, don't be greedy." He thrived on the action. Nothing seemed out of reach.

32

1967: The Summer of Love

1967 was aptly called The Summer of Love. "Hippies," young men and women with long hair, professed that peace and love would heal all troubles. During that memorable summer a hundred thousand young people, unorthodox in all ways and in all stages of dress and undress, consuming all types of drugs including marijuana and hallucinatory drugs, converged in the Haight-Ashbury area of San Francisco, California. Birth control pills had been approved by the FDA in 1960 and by the Summer of Love they had become a freeing phenomenon. These flower children wanted peace, not war, and staged massive protests against United States involvement in the Vietnam war. The wave of dissent continued to grow and young people were making their voices heard throughout America.

I stood firmly on the sidelines of the rebellion, an outsider of the social and political revolution exploding around the country. College graduation was imminent and my folks anticipated that I would proceed along a pre-determined path.

During that time the pressure for women to attain a college degree was equal to the push to find a marriageable suitor. Success at securing an "MRS" was considered a respectable and desirable college achievement. A career was almost a side note. Gainful employment options were limited for women. Those that pursued a college degree were directed to either teaching or nursing careers. Secretarial positions were acceptable, but primarily for those without four year degrees.

After two years at Arizona it was with mixed feelings that I approached graduation. Though I had blossomed like spring in the desert, melancholy swept over me. I was having the time of my life and I didn't want to leave. Some years later Mom remarked "I encouraged you to go away and you never came home again."

I walked the graduation line at University of Arizona though I still had to complete one more summer school class in San Diego. I moved back home and took the requisite Biology class with an eagerness to obtain my Bachelor of Science degree.

Avoiding thoughts of employment after graduation, my Arizona roommate, Harriet, a southerner from Arkansas, and I, made a plan to travel to Europe joining the popular trend of many of our contemporaries. I was aware that neither Mom nor Dad had ever been across the Atlantic and I expected considerable push back. I was right.

I chose a summer afternoon a few weeks after arriving home to approach the subject. "Mom and Dad, Harriet and I have a great idea. Before looking for a job we're going to travel through Europe this fall. Doesn't that sound great?" Silence. *Did they hear what I was saying?* Mom's expression changed from her usual smile to concern and the muscles in her neck tensed. She looked sideways to Dad. In a calm soft voice masking anxiety, she began, "You want to go to Europe? Young girls traveling alone? It's not safe." *I had prepared a thoughtful, steadfast, response.* "Everybody's going to Europe. I have my own money. I have $800 saved from birthday gifts and summer jobs. Why can't you just support me?"

Here I was, a 21 year old requesting the blessing of my parents at an age when Mom had become a bride. I nagged until they resigned themselves to the fact that I was an adult and I could not be dissuaded. I was going to Europe. They made two requests. "We want you to have an itinerary planned out, and check in at the American Express office in each country for mail." That I could agree to.

I was finishing that last class in Biology when I informed my instructor I was leaving for Europe as soon as the class was over. His note on my final paper summed it up beautifully. "Your knowledge of biology is lousy, but what the hell. When you're in Europe, go to the top of the Bavarian Alps and say OM three times and you will be absolved of your sins." And so I did....head to Europe.

Our Eurail passes led us on a six week journey from country to country. We had no responsibilities and had no concerns for the future. We used the five dollars allotted per day by sleeping on trains every few nights, then crashing at pensiones with bathrooms located down a dirty carpeted hall. We used hand gestures to ask for directions and held out our hands full of unfamiliar currencies to pay for transportation. My travels in Europe were as educational as the college degree I had earned over the past four years.

My enthusiastic letters and one phone call sparked Mom's and Dad's interest in traveling to Europe and beyond. I couldn't contain my excitement when calling home in the middle of the trip. I wanted to share a once in a lifetime experience and deemed it worthy of the $20 charge for a three minute long distance call to San Diego.

The black telephone rested in the cradle in the dark hallway between pensione rooms. There was a nine hour time difference between California and Vienna, Austria. I tiptoed into the dark hallway late at night and sat cross-legged on the dirty carpet. I whispered into the receiver trying not to wake other guests. "Hello, operator? Can you get me a line to the

United States? Yes, the United States. U.S.A. America. I-want-to-make-a-phone-call-to-San-Diego-California." Finally the operator, in heavy accented broken English responded, "Nur eine minute." I hung up and waited for the ring back. Finally, "Mom, Dad, are you there?" *c-c-r-ac-k-l-e, c-r-a-c-k-l-e*, "I'm in Vienna. (delay) Yes- Austria. (delay). Yes, I'm FINE. Everything is FINE. I am really here and tonight was so-o-o amazing. I went to a ballet starring Margot Fonteyn and Rudolf Nureyev. They were wonderful. It costs me twenty-six cents. Standing room."(delay) "Yes, Dad, it was worth all of the twenty-six cents."

This began my love of travel. Mom's push to go away to college had broadened my perspective far beyond the 400 miles to Arizona.

I returned home ready to move forward and find employment. My first job was as an Assistant Buyer in the lingerie department at Broadway Department Stores, a large retail chain. Earning a respectable salary of $110 per week, I was assigned to the large flagship store on the corner of Hollywood and Vine, in the heart of Los Angeles. I packed up, moved to West Los Angeles, and proceeded to rent an apartment with a high school friend. After merely one year I recognized that the path to a coveted buyer position was crowded with ambitious men. Equally important was that long retail hours cramped my social life. It was time to consider an alternate career.

"Why don't you go back to school?" Mom suggested. "Get your teaching credential. It's a great job for a woman and you'll always have something to fall back on." Though I wasn't sure if that was the right move, I quit my job, certain that retail was not going to be my chosen path.

Judy was gainfully employed as an elementary school teacher and had married Ed, a lawyer specializing in juvenile law. They settled in an apartment in Ocean Beach and lived a couple of miles from Mom and Dad where their lives crossed like an intersection in the busiest part of the city. "Ed thinks I live in the refrigerator," Dad joked. "Every time he comes over, he walks in the house, goes directly to the refrigerator, opens the door, and shouts 'Hi Sol'."

Merely one year after my European adventure Mom and Dad planned a trip abroad: to Rome, Paris, and Israel. They invited me to join them.

I was no longer employed. I was weighing my future options. Mom's words kept playing in my head as I drifted through a sea of possibilities, then was carried back by a wave of indecisiveness. But her voice made sense. "I really think you would like teaching and you'll have plenty of time off." So I made the easy decision and applied to University of Southern California for a one year program to earn a California Teaching Credential. There was enough time before school started to join Mom and Dad on their trip overseas.

The tiny country of Israel had gained independence just twenty years prior to our visit. Abandoned rusty tanks still remained on highway shoulders. The Israelis were passionate about their land as they struggled to survive and develop an infrastructure. Male and female soldiers carrying weapons were everywhere as were blue and white flags adorned with the Star of David. I was in the majority for the first time in my life.

We flew to Rome, visiting all the major sites, and then on to Paris, France. On a free afternoon strolling the streets of Paris, Mom and I proposed we separate from Dad for an hour to shop in the huge department store, Galleries Lafayette. My mission was to find another lacy black bra exactly like the one I had purchased the previous year. "Sol," Mom began "we're going to do a little shopping to get Suzi a special bra she wants. We will meet you at 3:00 on the corner of Boulevard Haussmann."

We lost track of time gawking at the Paris windows we passed after making our purchase. Mom glanced at her watch "Uh oh, we are late to meet Dad. We need to hurry. You know how nervous he gets." We arrived fifteen minutes late. There was Dad, grim-faced, hunched over on the street corner in his heavy jacket and hat. He was furious. "Why can't you be on time?" he fumed. "You always do this." In frustration, he threw down his hand, palm up "I was worried. I didn't know where you were."

He turned and walked towards an old stone building and leaned up against the cold mortar, a look of ire on his face. At that precise time a well-dressed Frenchman walked by. Thinking Dad, still with palm upright, was asking for money, the gentleman dropped a Franc in his upturned hand. Surprised, but still angry, he responded sharply "I'm NOT a beggar." The Frenchman simply walked on, accompanied by his small dog. We couldn't suppress our giggles - and Old Yeller, himself, had to laugh.

33

Los Angeles, California - 1969

Teaching second grade in the Los Angeles United School District pleasantly surprised me. Though I had been backed into a corner choosing this new career, I discovered it was rewarding to hear a seven-year-old sound out words phonetically and begin to find pleasure in reading. In addition, the pay was better than my retail job. Best of all, vacations and summers made it all worthwhile.

Though I now had time for a social life, meeting eligible men wasn't easy. Outside of the college environment, available men were nowhere to be found in my daily encounters. The elementary school staff was nearly void of single men. When I was not working I was mainly frequenting shopping centers and grocery stores. If I didn't meet a suitor in the produce department, the most viable way to meet a potential mate was on a blind date.

Blind dates in the late 60's were a precursor to the "swipe left, swipe right" tactic common today. Friends, relatives, co-workers, and everyone who knew anyone who was unattached, was always on the lookout to play matchmaker. A verbal promotional message, a Public Service Announcement (PSA), usually preceded a prospective date. "He has a good job." "He has a great sense of humor." "He loves dogs." Truthfully, it was a grab bag. The standard of the day was the belief that everyone needed to be married in order to be happy and fulfilled.

My boyfriends during high school and college were nice Catholic boys; fun to date. I had never dated any Jewish boys though I knew Mom and Dad expected me to marry someone of our faith. It should have been easy. I was living in LA, a city with a population of approximately a half million Jews. But I wasn't going to bars, didn't belong to a temple, and meet-up groups were decades in the future. The dating pool of single Jewish men just didn't intersect any part of my life.

I was willing to be fixed up with anyone who could check off a few desirable qualities on my wish list. All I was searching for was an educated, employed, energetic, adventurous, Jewish man with a good sense of humor.

The air surrounding most weddings invariably fogs up with feelings of love and romance. This is fertile ground for guests at nuptials to attempt recreational matchmaking. In early 1969, Steve and his wife, Barbara, traveled from their home in Los Angeles to attend a wedding in San Diego.

Steve had recently completed his military commitment in the Army. While serving overseas he had developed a close friendship with a draftee from the northwest. During the wedding reception Steve casually chatted with family friends who had known me from birth. "I know a great Jewish guy who just moved to L.A. I wish I knew someone to fix him up with," Steve mentioned coolly. The friends wasted no time. "Hey, we know a nice girl who just moved to L.A. also. I've got her number for you to give him." In the time it took for a quick sip of champagne, my contact information was passed on along with the cocktail appetizers.

While stationed in Vietnam, Steve met Chuck Gold in an unsuspected setting. The Cu Chi Army Base Camp for the 25th Infantry Division located in Tay Ninh, thirty five miles from Saigon, held Friday night Sabbath services for Jewish service members. This was not a well attended event on base. The number of participants varied from two to five including Steve and Chuck. Thus, at religious services far from home, these two men became fast friends.

After his discharge from the Army, Chuck returned to Seattle, Washington. Steve and Chuck had reconnected when Chuck accepted a job with Shell Oil Company, relocating to Los Angeles. A few days after Steve passed the tiny slip of paper with my contact information, Chuck took a leap of faith, picked up the phone, and dialed my number.

On February 1, 1969, a cold windy Saturday evening, the two of us stood in line outside a Westwood theater to catch a first run film. Earlier in the evening we had shared superficial talk over pizza at La Barbra's, a local restaurant. As we waited to buy tickets we bantered back and forth sharing information about our lives and our families. With a score of people lined up in front of us, Chuck volunteered information that added to the chill in the air.

"My family keeps kosher and I plan to keep kosher too." An alarm went off in my brain. I had never known anyone other than Dad's parents who kept kosher. In fact, I was raised in a family that enjoyed a baked ham on Christmas afternoon. I was dumbstruck. *Was he serious about that?* No details of the conversation that followed stayed with me. The true understanding of his statement was buried by the recognition that we had had a memorable fun first date that led to a second date the following day to the pier at Redondo Beach.

Chuck was unlike any other date I had been fixed up with. He was tall and muscular compared to my short stature, had beautiful blue eyes, was incredibly smart, extremely witty, had a great sense of humor, was fun to be with, and had a job - and he was Jewish.

At that point I thought "being Jewish was being Jewish." I had no idea. Though our values were similar, our history, as well as our religious observances, were dramatically different.

Mr. & Mrs. Charles Gold,
February 16, 1940

Chuck was born in France in the middle of World War II. His parents met in Belgium where his father was working as a jeweler and his mother went to visit her sister who was living there. They married on February 16, 1940.

Just two months later, on the morning of May 13, 1940, Charles and Anne Gold were forced to flee their home when the Nazis invaded. "We just closed the doors and left," Anne recalled. "We took only what we could carry." Hurriedly they boarded the train along with thousands of other refugees, hoping to travel to Paris then on to Spain. The train was stopped in Abbeville where they were ordered "Get off the train. It is needed to move the soldiers." They were surrounded by death when German planes dropped bombs around them.

The next year and a half was spent in small towns where Charles worked in vineyards and Anne sold jewelry she had brought from Belgium. In Bezier, France, they had a baby boy they named Claude, a good French name to help avoid suspicion of his Jewish birthright. Eventually they made their way to Malzuville, France, a town friendly to the Jews. The couple remained in hiding in the southern French city for the remainder of the war. A daughter, Marguerite, was born there and Anne and her children lived in a farmhouse while Charles was hidden in a convent. At the end of the war the family first went back to Belgium then four years later were sponsored by relatives and immigrated to New York then to Seattle.

Judaism was woven into the fabric of the Gold family and they continued to observe Orthodox traditions. Claude attended Jewish Day School that provided a strong course of study. Besides a well rounded and excellent education in all other subjects, he mastered Hebrew, stories from the Torah, and Jewish history. After attending public high school, Claude majored in Business Administration at the sprawling campus of University of Washington.

When his name conjured up a number of less than desirable monikers, Claude decided on a nickname, Chuck, a name as American as apple pie, then joined a fraternity. It was during his college years that he enjoyed his first "nonkosher" hamburger at the local hangout.

Seven years later Chuck had earned an undergraduate degree and an MBA. Congratulations came in the way of a letter from Uncle Sam. His student deferments had abruptly come to an end. He had been drafted, ordered to basic training at Fort Lewis, Washington, then on to Advanced Individual Training (AIT) at Fort Benjamin Harrison, Indiana, where he became a Postal Operations Instructor.

The unpopular war in Southeast Asia led many young Americans to flee to Canada to dodge the draft. But Chuck was ready to face the music. He turned down an offer to go to Officer's Candidate School to avoid an extended commitment and to stave off being sent to the conflict in Southeast Asia. He was 25 years old, older and more educated than most enlisted soldiers. When his orders came through, he learned, to his surprise, he was to be deployed to Vietnam. He was assigned to teach postal operations.

Though his parents had never discussed their war experiences with him, the untold stories and lack of grandparents and the few aunts and uncles who had survived,

Pvt E1- Chuck Gold
Fort Lewis
Washington, 1966

was enough evidence of the loss of family. Most of the extended family had perished in the Holocaust. Chuck headed to Vietnam wanting to prevent his parents from unnecessary worry. He bid them goodbye declaring he was being deployed - to Okinawa, Japan.

For months he sent letters home describing imagined weather, surroundings, and conditions of the island base. Then one day the truth was uncovered in a most unsuspecting manner. A postal worker noticed the cookies his mom was sending to an APO listed on the package. "Oh, I see your son is in Vietnam," the postman tried to initiate an innocuous conversation. "No!" his mom countered, her voice like a recently sharpen butcher knife. "That's not right. He is not in Vietnam. He's in Okinawa." "H-m-m-m" was all the postal worker responded, with his eyes focused downward. A day later, Chuck was summoned by a messenger. "Report to the CO immediately." "Call your mother - RIGHT NOW" the CO shouted. The truth was out, causing his folks anxiety until the day he was discharged and returned to Seattle in 1968.

Chuck had been raised in a traditional home but the main reason he attended Friday night Sabbath services 'religiously' while in Vietnam was a promise he had made to the Chief Warrant Officer. Upon arriving in Vietnam he was interviewed by CWO Sherman. "Are you Jewish?" the CWO asked, noting his last name. "Yes I am, sir." "Okay. If you can write a letter and will attend services on Friday evenings, I have a job for you." "Yes sir, I can and I will." He was assigned to serve as a Congressional Correspondent Clerk whose main job was to write letters for the Commanding Officer's signature, and every Friday night he had a commitment.

I knew nothing about an observant Jewish lifestyle. Keeping kosher? Separating meals and dishes for meat and milk? Avoiding shellfish and pork? On the contrary, I had been raised where religion governed our belief in one God but did not enter the kitchen. Now the differences in our Jewish lifestyles could practically qualify us as an "interfaith" couple.

After months of movies, restaurants, and meeting friends, I was anxious for Chuck to meet my family. We planned a Sunday afternoon excursion to Hemet, California. The town of Hemet is located slightly less than a hundred miles from Los Angeles and San Diego. It was a perfect meeting place and each May the town hosts a well known popular event. An outdoor stage performance of Helen Hunt Jackson's novel, "Ramona," is performed in the hills above the town. Hundreds of townspeople act in the play portraying either Native Americans or Mexicans, riding horses that kick up the dust behind the rocks and brush.

Prior to the performance we met for a picnic at the city park. I was excited and slightly nervous about introducing Chuck. I hoped the family would approve of my boyfriend. I felt for the first time *this might be my forever mate*. Mom, Dad, Judy, and Ed, greeted us and the conversation flowed easily as we ate our turkey sandwiches and drank our Cokes. Chuck's quick wit and sense of humor matched Dad's.

Dad eyed a chin-up bar on the nearby playground. He casually strolled over to the bar and claimed, "I think I can still do a chin-up." He reached up with his two middle fingers and wrapped them around the metal bar. He lifted his full weight up repeatedly with two-fingers. Chuck, twenty-something years younger, did his best to emulate his potential father-in-law. This fifty-one year old man had sent a message loud and clear "Don't mess with my daughter." It didn't stop him.

Chuck attempting to emulate Dad's
chin-ups, Hemet, CA 1969

34

He's The One

With boosted confidence Chuck approached Dad, "Sol, I want to ask you for your daughter's hand in marriage." Dad answered without hesitating, "You only want her hand? What about the rest of her?"

After a year of courtship we were ready to make a commitment for a lifetime together. We set our wedding date for the following summer of 1970. There was no doubt that we loved each other so we conveniently avoided the "elephant

Happily engaged, February 1, 1970

in the room." The fact that we were both Jewish should have been one less issue of concern, but the way we had each been raised crossed the spectrum of Judaism.

Mom's upbringing was displayed culturally; by actively living Jewish values of human rights and helping the less fortunate. In Judaism this is known as 'tikkun olam', which means to repair and improve the world. Traditional observances were limited to celebrating Jewish holidays and actively participating in non-profits that supported Jewish as well as non-Jewish causes.

On the contrary, Dad's Orthodox home adhered to Jewish laws written in the Torah, known as 'halakha,' guiding day-to-day living. Somehow, Mom and Dad had found common ground, and compromise that blended their backgrounds. *I wondered whether we could do the same.*

Mom stepped in to make all the wedding plans and arranged all the details from the food to the live music. That suited me fine. The only thing she couldn't do without me was choose my wedding gown. We spent an afternoon trying on dresses in the bridal department of an exclusive San Diego store when I slipped on a beautiful A-line sleeveless dress with lace covering the bodice. "This is the one. I love this dress." I gazed approvingly at myself in the full length mirror. Then I looked at the price tag. The gown was far over our budget so we politely exited the store telling the salesgirl, "That dress is beautiful but have a few more places to look before we decide."

On the way to our car Mom said cheerfully, "I think we can copy that dress perfectly and make it ourselves - just as beautiful." She wasted no time finding a pattern to adapt and ordered special lace from a fabric store our cousins in Salt Lake City recommended. On weekends I drove from Los Angeles to San Diego and we spent the days in the small alcove off the master bedroom sewing. Mom did the cutting, basting, and stitching on the machine while I focused on the handwork of appliqueing the lace across the bodice and skirt. The gown was perfect, but the treasured time Mom and I spent together on this labor of love was more meaningful than the dress.

For the next few months Chuck and I went about our jobs in Los Angeles. Chuck was still working in the Industrial Relations department at Shell Oil and was relocated to Ventura, California. I continued teaching second grade in Gardena, California.

Less than two months before the wedding, after a gleeful

engagement party and gift filled showers, we faced an impasse. Our religious differences bubbled to the top as volatile as a pot of boiling water. With no clear path to a resolution, we realized we needed space apart from each other to clear our heads. We went our separate ways; unsure whether the road ahead would eventually converge. *Should we cancel the wedding? How do we explain this to our guests? What about all the gifts?* I was spinning. My heart and my brain were on a collision path. I was feeling the sadness and the loss of a future we had talked about for months. I was raw to the bone - devastated.

When I broke the news to Mom and Dad they were, as always, there to console. They offered no advice, but suggested a creative diversion. Dad, an expert in denial, called. "I know just the thing to cheer you up," he offered, never mentioning Chuck or our break up. "We'll pick you up in L.A. and drive over to Las Vegas. Elvis is making his comeback at the International Hotel. How about it? Let's go see him?" In my sadness and confusion I understood that going to Las Vegas with Mom and Dad couldn't give me an answer. On the other hand, it couldn't hurt. I agreed to go. Besides, I loved Elvis.

They drove north to pick me up and the three of us made our way to Nevada. Hours later we arrived at the Sahara Hotel. "Where can we get tickets to see Elvis?" Dad asked as we checked in. He purchased the tickets and that evening we were off to see the King of Rock and Roll. The largest theater at the time in Las Vegas, accommodating 2,000 guests, was alive in anticipation.

The theater usher, looking like a member of the mafia in a dark suit and red tie, took our tickets. In an aloof no nonsense manner he led us to a table at the rear of the theater. Before we sat down Dad discreetly pressed a folded $10 bill in his palm "Do you have anything closer?" With a hand gesture indicating we should follow, we were shown a table rows closer to the stage. Minutes later Elvis swaggered onto the stage and broke out in song. His voice didn't fail as he belted out "Blue Suede Shoes." He continued his sensual lip-quivering performance for ninety minutes. There was no doubt that the King was again at the top of his game.

The evening had been spectacular and memorable, but it was only a temporary distraction from my doleful state of mind. *I love this man. Can I live without him? How can we find an acceptable compromise? We are a product of our backgrounds. How do we blend them?*

By the end of the weekend and after a few phone calls, Chuck and I had solved nothing but the weekend apart reconfirmed our desire to be together. Mom and Dad made no comments as they drove back to San Diego by way of Ventura and dropped me off at Chuck's apartment. They just cared about my happiness.

With the naiveté of youth, we again chose to ignore our situation. We were caught up in the romance of our impending wedding. A few weeks later, on August 16, 1970, we exchanged our vows at Temple Beth Israel, then celebrated at the Point Loma home Mom and Dad had now been living in for three years. It was still new enough that it was largely void of furniture. Dad had worked tirelessly to decorate the garage, converting it into a party room. With rented tables and chairs, a band on the patio, and caterers set up inside, we celebrated throughout the evening.

August 16th, 1970, we exchanged our vows at Temple Beth Israel

Following our honeymoon to Jamaica, we settled back into an apartment in Los Angeles. Wanting the honeymoon to continue, I agreed to support my husband's wishes. I would willingly maintain a traditional Jewish home. I would learn the blessing over the Sabbath candles and I would TRY to adhere to kosher laws. I was starting from the beginning - Kosher 101.

I was already at a disadvantage since I was an uninterested cook who was challenged in the kitchen. But I agreed to try. I would make an effort to keep a kosher home out of respect for Chuck, since he considered our marriage the beginning of his own family. Immediately I was stifled by the rules. No cheese on the chicken casserole? No butter on the baked potato with the steak? Where do I go to buy the kosher meat? My resolve only lasted a few weeks. I was cranky, unhappy, and felt that I was doing all the work for something I didn't believe in. In that short time we made a simple compromise that I could easily live with. We avoided all pork and shellfish in our home and went back to buying meat at the local supermarket.

Four years later Chuck was offered a promotion and a financial step up with Shell Oil. From Los Angeles we moved to Walnut Creek, a bedroom community across the bay from San Francisco. I got a job teaching and with two incomes and little responsibility we felt rich. We purchased a flashy orange Datsun 240Z for $4000 and crossed the Bay Bridge to the City by the Bay every weekend. San Francisco was intoxicating: drag shows, street fairs, Golden Gate Park, Haight-Ashbury, and sophisticated shopping. We proudly purchased our first home in Concord, California, and Mom and Dad traveled with old clothes packed, ready to help paint and make repairs on our home.

The next offer from Shell Oil, to the headquarters in Houston, Texas, was the end of living large. We couldn't imagine life in Texas and we had no interest in leaving California. Chuck turned down the promotion and jumped off the career ladder of Shell. Our future was now in limbo.

With no other opportunities at the forefront, Chuck accepted an offer from our matchmaker Steve, to sell life insurance in Los Angeles. We sold our house and headed back where we first fell in love and still had many good friends. Mom and Dad co-signed for a $24,000 two bedroom, one bath, home in West Los Angeles. In a few short weeks Chuck concluded, "I hate it. Insurance sales aren't for me." He was miserable.

Though we agreed he should quit, I was a few months pregnant and had a part-time job tutoring incorrigible kids who had been expelled from public high schools.

Chuck needed a job and we needed the income. He signed on for work that required none of his education skills - just muscle and perseverance. He accepted a route delivering the Los Angeles Times newspaper. The job lasted one long night as he lugged pounds of newsprint up and down staircases of multilevel L.A. apartment buildings. He arrived home, dragging and drenched in sweat at 6:00 in the morning, grabbed a beer, and stated emphatically, "I quit." He found work at a shoe store for two weeks and continued to apply for positions in his area of expertise, Human Resources. Finally hired in his field of knowledge, he began work in Anaheim at a company called CalComp. The position matched his experience, the salary was good, the traffic was awful. He immediately began to apply for positions closer to home.

On February 8, 1974, our perfect baby boy was born. We named him Joshua Riff, his middle name in honor of Chuck's mother's maiden name with the Hebrew name of Joseph, Chuck's grandfather. We felt that Josh's birth weight of 7 lbs. 11 oz., the same as Dad's Circle 7/11 Motel, was a good omen.

My Jewish education was again expanded when I learned that according to Genesis, the first book of the Old Testament, God instructed Abraham to circumcise himself and all his descendents. This is traditionally performed on the eighth day after a Jewish male is born. There was no question that Josh would have a circumcision ceremony, a 'bris', in the tradition of Jewish law.

Charles, my proud father-in-law, held Josh in his arms on the 'operating table'; the table we ate dinner off of each night. The mohel, the small, grey-haired, very senior man in the surgical mask, was to perform the circumcision on our newborn.

Josh, Balboa Park, San Diego 1976

Friends and relatives crowded around to celebrate this rite of passage. All the while Josh happily sucked on a wad of cotton drenched with wine.

The thought of the foreskin on my tiny baby boy being removed outside of a medical facility without a licensed doctor made me queasy. I couldn't witness the procedure, which in my mind could have been compared to major surgery. I hid myself in the bedroom until the quick process was over and it was time to partake in the delicious homemade pastries my mother-in-law had transported from Seattle. I was quickly learning about the tenets of Judaism.

Eight months after Josh filled our lives with joy, Chuck was hired by SONY Corporation at its new manufacturing plant in San Diego. It was destiny that the road led me full circle-back home to San Diego. I was thrilled to be home and closer to my family.

We purchased our third house in the planned community of Rancho Bernardo; happy to eliminate traffic with a five minute drive, almost a stones throw, from Chuck's work to home.

On April 10, 1977, we were thrilled with the birth of a beautiful baby girl weighing 6 lbs. 2 oz. We named her Lindsay after Lottie, my beloved grandmother. For no other reason than it sounded exotic and meant 'beloved' in French, we gave her 'Aimee' as a middle name. She was given the Hebrew name of Leah Rachel.

Lindsay was a happy baby with a sweet disposition. Even as a toddler, she idolized Josh, her big brother.

Our small family was growing. Dad's often repeated phrase "there's always room for one more" brought both Mom and Dad unparalleled joy. Judy and Ed's boys, Marc and Derek, and our children, Josh and Lindsay, completed our family of ten. They needed no instructions on how to dote on their four grandchildren. They realized their fortune. Their two children and four grandchildren were living close by.

Lindsay, 1977

35

From Generation to Generation

Visiting Nana and Papa was a 'Peter Pan' experience. Dad refused to grow old. He maintained the vibrancy, the spirit, and the vigor of youth. This drew the neighborhood kids, the housekeeper's daughters, the grandchildren and their friends, to Dad's overstuffed gameroom.

Previously a bedroom, the space was enlarged and converted to accommodate a seamless blend of the past and present. From floor to ceiling, memories of events overlapped with popular amusement games.

Grandchildren: Derek, Josh, Lindsay, Marc

White paneled walls were covered with multiple photos documenting our family history. Autographed pictures of celebrities lined up next to official documents; Dad's laminated discharge notice from the Army, his father's ragged peddler's license from Manchester, England. Souvenirs from overseas trips rested on shelves side by side with cast iron penny banks. Trendy pinball machines, arcade games, and antique slot machines framed the perimeter of the room with a bumper pool and an air hockey table in the center. On a corner table near the gumball machine serving as the base of a lamp rested a working Mickey Mouse telephone. This was Dad's museum of memories. The cost of entrance for any of the kids or adults who stepped in was merely a smile. The gameroom blended the past with present day amusements,

Prominently in the corner stood the "Chief." The life-sized carved Native American chief, adorned with a feathered headdress and tomahawk, was complete with a working antique slot machine set in his belly. This was Dad's gift to himself on his 80th birthday. "Why in the world did you buy that?" everyone asked. He had a simple answer. "All my life I've wanted an 'Indian' with a slot machine for a stomach." That was a good enough reason.

Most adults who entered the house had a hard time resisting the urge to spend a few minutes in this land of entertainment. Even the most blasé of visitors usually pulled a slot machine handle a few times hoping for nickels or quarters to drop down.

As they got older and had favorites, the grandchildren jostled for position. "It's my turn on Ms. Pac-Man." "I get the baseball machine first."

The Chief

After a few minutes rotating games, we would hear a loud high-pitched voice, "Pop, the quarter's stuck. Can you come fix the slot machine?" Dad would take the back off the machine, clear the jam of quarters while repeating with mild annoyance, "Only one quarter at a time. You can't keep putting in quarters without pulling the handle each time." Dad was in his element in this room, long before the term 'Man Cave' was

171

ever coined. Though no monetary value could be estimated on his collection, these were Dad's priceless treasures.

Dad was a bigger than life force, but Mom was "Elmer," the family glue. She took her job as mediator and ambassador for the family seriously. When we had complaints about family members, friends, work, or kids, she listened patiently. She let us vent, then offered rational advice about which battles to choose. She was the ultimate diplomat; always ready with a 'peace pipe'. She possessed the quiet strength of Hercules combined with the brightness of a rainbow following a rainy day. We expected that our Pollyanna would be there forever to keep the peace, but all too soon we would find out otherwise.

36

The New Decembers

As life whooshed by we marked the years with minor ups and downs, though mainly with the joy of everyday living that meant seeing the family often and communicating by phone on a daily basis.

Each of the four grandchildren, now teenagers, held a unique place in their grandparent's heart. Pop approached Marc's homework projects as if he himself was working towards a high school diploma. Derek exhibited athletic ability in team sports, and Mom and Dad blended in with parents in the bleachers cheering him on. Josh was the family comedian. "That's a good one" Pop chuckled, delighted in his grandson's quick wit and ever-ready jokes. Lindsay, nicknamed Lulu, sweet and loving, touched everyone with her happy disposition and ready hugs.

The grandkids knew that Nan and Pop's home always had an open door and there were plenty of enticing attractions to keep them amused. They played pinball and Donkey Kong, shot

Josh's Bar Mitzvah. February 7, 1987

baskets at the hoop on the driveway, watched TV, etc.

The three boys designated Lulu as their security guard. She was a people pleaser and took her assignment seriously. They discovered the Playboy Channel with voluptuous 'Bunnies', available on the small television in Nan's sewing alcove. Lulu served as the lookout, scouting for any adult headed towards the back bedroom. "Here comes Nana! Hurry, change the channel." Lindsay ran back to warn the boys, though not always in the nick of time. "Now boys!" Nan would admonish and change the channel while the boys laughed and tried to blame each other.

The seasons flowed from one to the next, from the heat of summer to the refreshing breeze of fall to the California sun and gray of winter. With the changes in the air, so came changes in our family celebrations. The month of December was no longer consumed with operating the Christmas tree business that had been a memorable part of my childhood. Dad's multiple tree lots in the business he had truly loved were no longer profitable and viable. After years of December pandemonium, the month was now void of the ebullient chaos we had all enjoyed.

From the first year of marriage Chuck had annually excused himself from Christmas morning at Mom and Dad's, where a tinsel draped fir was surrounded by piles of gifts bearing decorative labels with names for each member of the family. I adored our Christmas celebration: the smell of the tree, opening the presents we had given and received, and the afternoon where friends and neighbors dropped by our house for drinks and sweets.

But there was no denying that the climate was changing. I was married, now one half of an equal and loving partnership, and a mother. I was beginning to view my Judaism from a different perspective. The festivities that I had encroached on and had enjoyed had begun to feel strangely awkward, as if I was borrowing something valued without asking permission.

I respected Chuck's strong mind, his pride in his heritage, his comfort in his skin. We needed to raise our children in agreement, as one unit.

I would not act as a hybrid any longer-trying to blend Judaism with Christianity like a mixed cocktail that is out of balance. I was learning to enjoy Christmas cheer with friends who could rightly claim ownership on the holiday, without borrowing the commercialism as my own.

Comfortable with my conviction, I was also aware I had upset a Schultz family tradition, one that the rest of the family eagerly participated in. Mom and Dad were caught in the middle, between continuing the way Christmas had been celebrated for years with half the family, or finding an alternative to fill the space.

We continued to celebrate the Jewish holidays together. We gathered for Passover, Rosh Hashanah and Yom Kippur, and to light the menorah during Chanukah.

Celebrating Rosh Hashanah with Mom and Dad -1987

Since schools usually closed for two weeks during December and workloads were minimal for everyone, Mom and Dad suggested that the time off was perfect for a getaway. Our one day excursions began with Disneyland, Universal Studios, then Knotts Berry Farm. Within a few years the adventures were extended to a few days when we drove to Arizona or Palm Springs. These getaways became an annual outing that we all looked forward to. They grew in length and dimension. "How about going to Hawaii? We'll take everybody for a week," Mom and Dad proposed. After a few of these excursions there seemed to be an acceptance that the joy of Santa was no more pleasurable than a week of over indulgence.

Our multi-generational family was now defined in three categories: youth, middle age, and senior citizens. Cruising seemed to be a perfect option to please our range of ages. Our itineraries were driven by warm weather: Mexico, the Caribbean, and the Bahamas. Each cruise included at least one or

Marc, Josh, Lindsay, Derek

two days at sea. Dad preferred the days at sea more than the days in ports. During the leisurely afternoons when many cruisers were at leisure resting on deck chairs, Dad was entering competitions, befriending the stewards, waiters, entertainers, activity staff, or making conversation with other passengers. He encouraged us to participate with him. "Who wants to go with me and enter the shuffleboard contest?"

Mom & Dad win 1ˢᵗ prize in the costume parade on a cruise

His favorite on-board event was the costume parade. "I packed the two–headed Arab and Mom brought her belly dancer outfit," he announced after embarking. On the following cruise he took the "three legged man" costume then on the next one he packed the "bag lady" outfit. He portrayed "William Tell" one year, his costume completed with a fake arrow that "pierced" his head. The gold plastic trophies he won were displayed proudly on the shelves of his game room; "1st Place Costume Parade," "Winner Shuffleboard Contest," or something of equal status.

On the first day of each cruise Dad gave each of the grandchildren a $20 bill with instructions, "Spend this any way you want." The ship's casino was enticing for these teenage gamblers. The evening at the casino would be summed up the next morning by one or the other. "I was up $10.00 then lost it. I'm pretty sure I'll make up for it tonight. I'm feeling lucky."

Marc had discovered that no cash was required at the bar in the disco. He could easily sign his name and cabin number to pay for drinks. He generously treated new friends each night. "Just charge it to my room," Marc directed the bartender. It was discovered on the last day of the Caribbean cruise when settling up the bill at the purser's office. The total bar bill for Marc's stateroom was almost equal to the cost of the cruise. That loophole was closed by the next cruise.

37

Begin Again

For twenty-five years Dad relished his days at the Circle 7/11 Motel. Truthfully, he was more than Sol Schultz, partner and General Manager. He was the mayor of this motel. He was a windup toy, moving nonstop around the office and premises to keep the 'machine' well oiled and running smoothly. The motel was in Mission Valley, convenient for family members to drop by for lunch at Ricky's on the way to or from most destinations in San Diego.

The entire family learned to scribble *Sol Schultz*, charging the restaurant bill to Dad no matter who we were with, knowing he was happy to treat us.

Once in a while I phoned Dad at the motel proposing "Hi Pop, I am coming to the Valley on Friday. Wanna go to lunch with me? Ricky's of course. How about 12:30?" "Sure baby. I'll take you to lunch," he responded enthusiastically. On arrival I found Dad in his office. He welcomed me with a kiss and acknowledged everyone in our path as we walked next door to the restaurant. "Hey Claude, Suzi and I are here for lunch" he acknowledged the owner behind the register. Claude directed us to a booth, handing us the menus we could practically recite by heart. "Marge, how is your kid doing in school?" Dad greeted a waitress on the way to our seats.

Dad treated the staff at the motel and restaurant more like friends than employees. He took it upon himself to know about family members: who had a son applying to college, who had a sick spouse, and who had just become a grandparent. His concern even spilled into the area of spirituality when he advised Jane, a middle aged waitress who had a desire to convert to Judaism. She expressed her appreciation in a book she presented to Mom and Dad. "If it were not for the help of the both of you, my true dream of becoming a Jewish woman would never have been this soon...Thank you both for the true-sincere beautiful friendship."

Once our lunch order was taken and Dad had asked "So what's new?" his eagle eyes locked on a table of unsuspecting diners across the room. "I'll be right back, baby." He offered no explanation as he made a beeline to the opposite side of the restaurant. I sat awkwardly solo until two plates of food were set down at the table. I watched him float around the room chatting with tourists, employees, old friends and new acquaintances, as if he were the maître d' at a fine restaurant. After taking each bite slowly, and finishing the last few chips on my plate, Dad would remember I was there and head back to our table with a predictable question, "So how was your sandwich?"

Every family member had the same complaint. "Pop, we came to eat the lunch with you, not by ourselves." But we learned not to take it personally for it was not personal.

Dad had no desire to retire in 1990, but he was not given a choice. The major partner in the Circle 7/11 Motel decided to sell the property. In the blink of an eye, Dad was ousted from this home away from home. He suddenly found himself to be a 'fish out of water'. But Dad was a 'do-er' and he was ready to reinvent himself-once again.

"Sol, do whatever you want, just don't plan to be home

for lunch" was Mom's only request. He had no designs on cramping Mom's lifestyle. With a desire to catch up in the age of technology, he registered for an adult education course called "Learning the Computer for Seniors." The attempt was unsuccessful because he could not grasp the idea that a computer could accomplish so many functions with a few pecks on a keyboard.

He had always been comfortable writing longhand in his trademark scribble or using the two finger hunt and peck method on a typewriter, and calculating on an oversized adding machine. He could see and touch all his saved receipts, notes, and printed copies of important documents. He placed these in labeled manila folders in a file cabinet or in Xerox boxes that were lined up in the garage.

In retirement he found the time again to write, like he had done throughout his college years. When he signed up for an adult writing class he took another leap of faith and purchased a data processor. He was amazed that words could be moved around, grammar and spelling corrected, and sentences erased without using Wite-Out. He called his Brothers word processor "just marvelous."

At seventy-two Dad joined a senior baseball team and played racquetball at the high school gym. On the field and off he lived by his motto, "I'm not out yet. I'm on third base and I'm coming up to bat again."

Growing cymbidium orchids surprisingly became a passion that would not have been predicted. Dad coddled and nurtured each plant with parental attention and concern. He occasionally gifted us with a plant then followed it up with a lecture. "You need to fertilize the orchid. If it gets too big for the pot, you need to split it. If you don't know how, bring it back to me and I'll do it for you." The few pots multiplied to dozens after he fastidiously split, fertilized, re-potted, watered, and proudly displayed the stately flowers in rows as if each flowering stalk was in competition for a blue ribbon in the county fair flower show.

Dad spent time at his workbench in the garage adjusting watchbands to help a flight attendant friend who often traveled in Asia. On her layovers in the Far East she purchased replicas of well known designer watches: Rolex, Cartier, etc. She sold these watches for a small profit back home in San Diego. The metal bands on these watches were invariably too long for the buyers. Between assignments Mary brought the watches to Dad who sat at his workbench with a spotlight shining on each watch. He carefully worked the tiny tools he had acquired to make adjustments as if he was making repairs on fine jewelry. It made no difference that the watches were fakes or whether they kept accurate time. Mary needed help and he was happy to assist.

Magic had intrigued Dad as long as I can remember. He was awed by it all: illusions, sleight of hand, close-up magic. He never passed up a visit to a magic shop, buying trick card decks, scarfs, rings that hooked together, and thrived in the magic lessons we gave him one year for this birthday. He found the perfect audience in Judy's third grade classroom. He was delighted when she invited him to perform each year.

"Choose a card, any card, and stick it anywhere in the deck" he directed an eight year old who would break out in gales of laughter when Dad managed to turn up the correct card from the deck. When Dad magically pulled a penny out of the ear of a pigtailed girl he felt like David Copperfield. He loved entertaining but he was smart enough never to try to make a living as a magician.

Mom had her own interests. Besides weekly Bridge and Pan games and her volunteer work, she excelled in handiwork. She created jewelry with semi-precious beads, mastered knitting, and made clothing for the children so expertly that they were

Mom shows off her gymnastic skills

saved in boxes long after they were outgrown. Even with stains or moth holes they could never be parted with, for these were a labor of love. When she gifted us with one of her masterpieces, she always proclaimed "It's cheaper than a therapist and I get more joy." Mom could still impress us by performing a throwback from her youth by standing on her head at picnics or when challenged by her grandkids.

Dad was hurrying to find new activities in retirement while Mom kept a slow and steady course. Her main occupation was still serving her "country" of ten. She was the Secretary-General of our own United Nations.

38

Food for Thought

Mom and Dad were like night and day. She was the peanut butter to his jelly, yin to his yang. He was loud and boisterous. Her manner was cheerful, warm, and welcoming. He was the building blocks, she was the foundation. And their marriage worked. Their opposite personalities, likes and dislikes, seemed to fit together like a thousand piece puzzle that took energy, time, and focus.

Dad had no appreciation for gourmet food. This was a good thing. In spite of Mom's creativity, the kitchen was not her creative studio. Dad had a few favorite meals that Mom prepared: shepherd's pie, porcupine meatballs, and beef stroganoff. But he was as happy with an Arby's roast beef sandwich as a home-cooked meal. It was as an adult that I discovered there were more varieties of cake than chocolate and vanilla and that all cakes didn't come out of a box requiring the addition of two or three ingredients.

In reality Dad was a "nosher," a junk food lover. Not Mom. She never deviated from three meals a day plus an afternoon snack. Her late day go-to was one of two treats. Sometimes she nibbled on a square of buttered matzo with a small glass of Manischewitz, the unleavened cracker and sweet wine used during the Passover Seder. More often Mom savored a cup of hot tea and a single piece of See's candy.

During her healthy years, her nightly ritual was consistent. An avid reader, Mom settled into bed each night with a good book or magazine. On the shelf of the headboard behind her she set a glass of water along with a Navel orange that had been cut into quarters. Engrossed in her book, a nightlight shined on the written words. Dad, his rhythmic snoring filling the quiet space, was sound asleep beside her. With one hand she gingerly reached up to retrieve the glass of water from the headboard. Occasionally her grasp was not secure, dumping the glass of water on Dad's dream-filled head, drenching him and the sheets. "Je-e-e-sus Christ Charlotte, you did it again!" Dad shouted his regular phrase of outrage. This sent Mom into gales of laughter, who was joined by Dad after he calmed down, wiped his face, and changed his pajamas.

One of Dad's favorite pastimes was going out to lunch or dinner at local restaurants. He preferred the all-you-can-eat, soup to nuts, buffets. Surely the food was not the draw. The set-up and multiple food stations allowed Dad to easily circulate the restaurant and work the room, interacting with as many customers as possible. He perused the tables on the way to the buffet line, looking for targets. With each trip to refill his plate, he would hesitate at any table where he could catch a friendly smile. "Hey, I like your shirt. I see you're a Charger fan, huh?" "Hey little guy. That's a lot of food. Are you gonna be able to eat all that?" He was never short of words. It made no difference who the victims were.

One evening Chuck and I accompanied Mom and Dad to Hometown Buffet, his favorite eating establishment. Upon entering, we encountered an exceptionally long line of customers waiting to pay before being seated. Dad, in his late 80's, began a conversation with a gentleman about the same age standing ahead of us in line. He was accompanied by his adult daughter. Father and daughter waited patiently, speaking softly to each other.

Dad stepped in closer "Pretty long line, huh? Well, the food's pretty good so it's worth it." The father/daughter couple smiled and shook their heads in agreement. Dad found no need to wait for a response. He continued with superficial pleasantries. Then he began "Did you hear about the priest and the rabbi who got in a car crash?" He began to tell one of his favorite jokes - and one of the few he could still remember. When he got a giggle from his "audience" he was on a roll. The jokes went on for the next ten minutes. When we finally stepped up to the cashier we were informed, "The young lady in front of you paid for your dad's dinner. She said that she and her father appreciated that your dad had entertained them as they waited."

Years later, Dad and Mom, both in wheelchairs, joined by two caregivers, became weekly regulars at a popular woodfire pizza chain. Always cold, summer or winter, they were both bundled up in heavy jackets. Dad, still sharp of mind, and Mom, in the fog of dementia, would be rolled through the restaurant door to their usual table. Dad had befriended the manager. Seeing them enter, the manager rushed over to greet the party. "Hi Sol. Glad to see you. How ya doin' today?" Dad proceeded to tell a joke, possibly one he had told the week prior.

One day he questioned the manager "Hey Joe, why don't you put avocado in the salad? I love 'em. They'd add a lot to the salad." From that point on, whenever Dad and his caregivers crossed the threshold of the restaurant, the manager hurried to the grocery store a few doors away to buy an avocado, bring it back, and add it to Dad's salad. When Joe moved on he passed this direction on to the succeeding manager.

The caregivers particularly enjoyed these outings, ordering right to left from the menu without limitations. When the bill was dropped on the table, one of the caregivers reached into Dad's pocket, got out his credit card and figured the tip. Without looking at the charges, Dad scribbled his signature on the bottom. The man who saved every receipt to check the accuracy against his credit card statement each month didn't bother and didn't care anymore.

39

Seniors Entertaining Seniors

Life had gotten in the way of Dad's playwriting since his college days. For fifty years he had mostly written love letters and poems to Mom like the one following, presented on an anniversary when Mom was still capable of buying something for herself.

I tried to buy a present - as different as could be!
A mink you got, and jewels a lot - I had a problem - see?
At last I had a thought - A painting for the house.
By Rembrandt, Dali, Rubens - Or even L Toulouse.
I wrote and asked the gallery where I could buy just one.
What they wrote back I wouldn't say - even only in fun.
At last I found just what I thought would answer my request
A small engraving of Franklin - the U.S. treasury's best.
Love for many years. Sol

Now he had the time. He could again pursue his love of writing plays and participating in the theater. He joined the "Golden, Not Over the Hill, Players."

These thespians were, in fact, "over the hill." The cast of actors, dancers, and singers, were between the ages of 50 and 85. Without exception, they were young at heart with a love of theater. Their leader, Carlyn, was an enthusiastic ball of energy who encouraged and praised each performer. It was questionable whether any of the participants had enjoyed a successful career in theater. Some of the entertainers had notable talent. Without exception, all were there for the fun of it.

In his mid 80's, Dad's affinity to this close knit group sparked new vigor and sense of purpose. Mom participated also, though it was recognized she was losing some of her sharpness. She didn't possess the liveliness, the awareness, or the camaraderie that Dad enjoyed. Mom was most often in the background with a walk-on role that she could handle.

These seniors wrote, choreographed, and practiced for months, then took their shows to nursing homes, senior residences, and senior centers. Many of the actors were as old as those they entertained. In the nursing homes caregivers rolled the elderly in wheelchairs to the community room. Other residents shuffled in, leaning on their walkers. Some gray heads in the audience nodded off mid show. Others stared blankly, not comprehending the skits though were mindlessly aware of the activity before them.

About two times per year these thespians would perform on stage for friends and family. The rousing applause gave the Players all the encouragement they needed to feel this was a worthwhile pursuit. Though Dad couldn't hear the actors recite their lines and he couldn't sing or dance, he excelled in enthusiasm and spirit. He was often designated as the Master of Ceremonies. "Welcome everyone to the Golden Hill Players. My name is Sol. I was given my name by my mother at birth. When she first took a look at me, she shouted 'That's all'. So the nurse wrote down Sol on my birth certificate...." His monologue was rewarded with laughter.

Many of the skits Dad wrote were performed by the actors. Dad beamed from the audience as "The Ark," a modern day spoof on the tale of Noah's Ark was one of the skits performed. "Sophie's Coming to Dinner" was a humorous story about a Jewish family whose daughter, under pressure to date a Jewish man, brings a pseudo date, someone hired to fake the qualifications expected of Sophie's date, to dinner. "Sophie" was selected to be read at a local coffee shop. Dad's expression as the story was interpreted by professional actors was comparable to a parent proudly observing his child receiving an award at an elementary school.

Mom and Dad's tradition of 'adopting' people included the "Not Over the Hill Players." Their old friends had become less active and less social. Dad invited the Players to their home. Some joined us at our family Thanksgiving dinner. At Dad's request, we included a couple of the entertainers in our Passover Seder, Jews and non-Jews alike.

In a letter written to Reader's Digest Dad stated *"I do MC and standup comedy which job I got by default. Default was I couldn't sing or dance or play a musical instrument, but jokes and stories I have been telling since I was a student at San Diego State College. I am enclosing jokes I have told and other items you may be able to use. If you can't use them I won't feel bad..."*

He never heard back, but this did not discourage him from continuing to write and perform.

40

What a Shopper

"Charlotte, I'm going shopping. Do you want me to get anything for you?" Dad was headed to one of his favorite stores. A chosen avocation in retirement became searching for bargains. Pic 'N' Save, Costco, The Dollar Store, and the 99 Cent Store were his domain. At every visit to any of these locations his shopping basket overflowed with a variety of products. He explored each and every aisle like an archeologist digging to unearth an undiscovered treasure.

These outlets carried food and household goods sold at major discounts. We often discovered that the products didn't live up to their promotional ads. The votive candles with very short wicks were difficult to light, the snack food was sometimes discontinued by the manufacturer, and the holiday items were often still on the shelf after the celebrated date had passed.

Invariably, a variety of cookies graced the end cap topped with a sign promoting an "Unbelievable Low Price." Dad couldn't resist loading a bunch of packages of these cookies, even when he could feel some broken pieces within the wrapper. He couldn't pass up an animal shaped flashlight, a sports related bobble head of a has-been celebrity, collectible pins from the last Olympics, or Halloween candy sold in November. Like milk and cookies left for Santa, Dad gave these treats year round for anyone and everyone he encountered.

Though he was a discerning shopper, Dad never bought anything for himself. "I don't need anything. I have everything I want" he told us when we asked for gift suggestions. Thus, he assumed false delight in every gift we bestowed on him. "Oh, boy. That's terrific," he graciously acknowledged the giver. A few minutes later there was always a follow-up "Hey, how much did that cost? Do you have the receipt?" He usually – always - returned the gift. The only thing he kept was the closet full of sweaters and shirts Mom bought him and insisted he keep. He hated waste and excess, living by his own rule "If you haven't used it in six months, dump it!"

Each December Dad prepared a special treat as a holiday gift. Hershey's Gold Almonds were five individually gold wrapped candy bars packed in a decorative box. Not available in stores locally, they had to be ordered directly from the Hershey Company in Hershey, Pennsylvania. "Huki, will you order the candy for me?" Dad requested of my sister each year. When the huge carton was delivered he asked her to make twenty individual baskets filled with the candy bars. Dad would spend weeks before Christmas delivering these baskets to bank tellers, barbers, the accountant, postman, etc. His reputation for these chocolate bars spread. It was years after Dad's passing when his dermatologist's wife asked Judy "Hey, do you still get the Hershey bars?" That sweet memory lived on.

Dad's specialty, and his only foray into the kitchen, was in the fall when he made what we deemed his award winning caramel covered apples. He created these step by step, first thrusting wooden popsicle sticks into tart green apples. Judy and I were responsible for unwrapping the sticky caramel squares and placing walnuts in the nut chopper. We took turns crunching the nuts. Then Dad placed the caramel into the double boiler stirring the candy until it melted and became smooth and thick. He grabbed the apple by the stick and gently rolled it in the caramel then rotated it in the bowl of chopped nuts. The apples were set to cool on waxed paper, then cut in pieces. With the first bite, the sweet juice from the apple dripped down the corners of our mouths as the sticky candy adhered to our teeth. With jaws clenched, we struggled to separate our upper and lower molars as we relished the contrast of the sweet candy blending with the juicy apple.

In later years when this annual tradition became too laborious, Dad discovered a gourmet shop where he could purchase the apples already coated with nuts and candy. "I need you to drive me to La Jolla. I need to get something," he told the caregivers or one of us. He usually left the store with a dozen or more apples, each costing about five dollars. He proudly shared these among the family. Though they were delicious, they never reached the perfection of Dad's mouth-watering treats.

Mom and Dad's generosity to us and the grandchildren was abundant. They chose to gift us while they were alive and could watch us enjoy it. There were no strings attached to the gifts.

Their kindness extended far beyond the family. They continued to give both of their time and money. When the Kidney Foundation needed a Master of Ceremonies, or COMBO (Combined Arts and Education Council of San Diego) needed an auctioneer, Dad was ready to step up. If the Temple needed new air conditioning, Mom and Dad could be counted on to contribute.

Auctioneering was an art to Dad and he was the artist. "Sold!" he would exclaim after driving up an auction price by encouraging competing bidders. "We're doing a terrific job raising money for a great cause. I hear $500 for this --, do I hear $600?"

Dad, the COMBO auctioneer at Hotel del Coronado 1972

When the bidding was over, he often had one more trick. "Thank you to the winner, number 46, and to our generous benefactors, Mr. and Mrs. ---, for donating — to this worthwhile cause. We were able to raise quite a bit of money for the charity. Mr. and Mrs. ---, are you here? There you are. Is there any possibility that we could get you to generously provide one more of the same gift at the same winning bid?" Dad's ploy most often worked.

The Women's Domestic Abuse Shelter run by Catholic Charities in downtown San Diego was Dad's favorite cause and charity. He collected clothing from Mom's affluent friends, encouraging them to donate their gently used designer suits, elegant dresses, pants, and blouses. Dad filled trash bags with these clothes, loaded up his car, and dropped them off at the shelter

One day I drove Dad and a carload of clothing to the shelter. I double-parked in front of the building and the women inside ran out to greet us. "Hi Mr. Schultz. It's good to see you. What have you got for us today?" The women gave Dad warm and appreciative hugs then carried the bags of clothing inside the shelter. When the supervisor told Dad that clothing donations were plentiful but rarely included underwear, he took it to heart. A couple of times a year he headed to WalMart and bought a few dozen pairs of underpants, granny style, to distribute to the women.

Through hard work and a life of living within their means, Mom and Dad were financially comfortable. They had all they needed and wanted.

Their one splurge was Mom's car, a sporty Cadillac Seville. The soft lavender exterior body was complete with a white hardtop. Mom could barely see over the steering wheel, even with the electronic seat adjusted to the highest level possible. Dad lovingly bought a cushion for her to place on the seat giving her needed lift. She loved that car though she only drove a few thousand miles each year. Dad added a personalized license plate declaring "Wot-A-Joy" to the classy ride. Then he added a license plate with "Thatsol" on his beloved Camry. When Mom could no longer drive, the car, years old, was donated to Jewish Family Services with about 50,000 miles on it. It had barely been broken in.

Mom and Dad did not take their good fortune for granted. Mom would often declare, "Life is a great equalizer - sometimes you are up and sometimes you are down." Their life was full and they were happy with their lot. I fooled myself into believing that their energy, health, and zest for life would go on forever.

41

Wake Up Call

It was a milestone for our family that by 1999 all four grandchildren had earned their college degrees. Marc, the eldest, had graduated from University of Southern California, then Derek from University of Arizona and Josh from University of California at Santa Barbara. The youngest of the grandchildren, Lindsay, earned a Bachelor of Science degree in Social Work, graduating from University of California at Berkeley.

Mom, Lindsay, and me
Tri Delt Mother/Daughter luncheon
UC Berkeley, March 1997

Lindsay's degree suited her personality and kind nature. But after spending two years helping the homeless population in San Francisco her thirst for adventure prompted her to change her direction. There was no better place to offer a carefree life than in Hawaii. She and her college friend packed up, headed to Maui, and rented an apartment close to the beach. Her job as a cocktail waitress allowed her to work well after the midnight hour, sleep all morning, and play at the beach all afternoon.

We accepted her wanderlust but missed her being thousands of miles away. In 2001 we booked a flight to Maui to get a firsthand look at her island life. Chuck and I were delighted when Mom and Dad agreed to join us. We arrived in Maui as the sun shone a bright clear yellow, the sky was a pure blue, and the elephant ear shaped red anthurium flowers lined the airport walkways. Exiting the airport, the tropical breeze spread the sweet smell of plumerias. This really was paradise.

We drove our rental car to Lindsay's apartment. Mom seemed dazed. Her eyes clouded, a confused look of "Where am I?" spread across her face. "Mom, we're here in Hawaii to visit Lindsay. Are you okay?" We sensed her bewildered state when Lindsay greeted each of us with a hug. "Oh-h-h" she mumbled. "Oh, hi Lindsay." In silence we each pondered as to whether she even recognized her beloved granddaughter. We guided her to a chair as she shuffled haltingly, unsteady on her feet. There was no denying it. At that precise moment in time we each recognized something extraordinary and troubling was happening to the woman whose stature was much larger than her petite frame. *What was going on? Did she take too many headache pills? Or was this something else - something more foreboding?* During the days that followed, Mom's inability to enter into a meaningful conversation or recognize where we were was unsettling. She followed our lead, not participating, not comprehending. She moved along but it was obvious she was out of touch, in a fog.

One morning Dad and I walked together along the boardwalk of Kaanapali Beach. Luxurious high-rise hotels clustered together dwarfed us on our right side and carefree vacationers splashed in the crystal warm waves beyond the fine white sand on the left side. Though we walked side by side, we were alone with our thoughts.

Dad, his low, troubled voice quaking, began "I don't know what to do. I am so worried about Mom. She repeats the same stories over and over, she forgets what I tell her, her eyes no longer sparkle, and she sometimes acts like a little kid. I don't know what is happening to her. I don't know how to help." I had no words to console him. I had no words to make it better. "Dad, I know. I am worried too." While the sun's rays glistened on the Pacific Ocean and the surfers crested on the breaking waves, tears rolled down Dad's cheeks. Bit by bit he was losing his soulmate. Like the sand of Hawaii, Mom was sifting through our fingers.

The beauty of Maui was obscured by the reality of this pivotal moment. The future had become hazy and there was a new normal, or abnormal, for Dad and all of us. Mom, the quiet and unassuming backbone of the family, was no longer recognizable. The torch she carried with grace dimmed more each day. It would be passed on though it would never again would be as bright as when Mom carried it. We had crossed a line in the sand. It had become more than just a visit with Lindsay. It was the "before and after." We had begun the long good-bye.

42

One Last Time:
Branson, Missouri - 2005

"T----rific, t---rific! Whata show! Whata show!" Dad bubbled with enthusiasm as he approached the Dean Martin impersonator. We had just watched the production of "The Rat Pack Live Tribute" and as soon as the applause died down, Dad stood up and, in a slow gait, walked towards the stage. He had something important to say to Dean.

This was our third show in two days in the city known for: 100+ live shows, 200 places to stay, and tourists with blue hair, no hair, and on Medicare. THIS was Branson, Missouri. Dad and Mom had been to Branson years prior and considered it the most enjoyable destination in America. Dad's wish was to travel to Branson "one more time." They were in their mid eighties. There was no way they could travel without help.

Mom's confusion was much more noticeable and she was unable to function on her own. Her memory was seriously compromised though she showed no agitation, being her usual sweet self. Dad's enthusiasm definitely exceeded his physical ability necessary to coordinate the details of travel.

I couldn't talk any other family member into going with me but Lindsay, my go anywhere, go anytime daughter, had returned to the mainland to get a master's degree. She agreed to join me on this adventure to help navigate through the Bible Belt of Missouri.

On the stage were three actors/singers who performed as the Rat Pack, impersonating Sammy Davis Jr., Frank Sinatra, and Dean Martin. With the help of a staff of stylists, make-up artists and hairdressers, this trio physically resembled the real performers. They brought back fond memories of a bygone era to the aged audience. Actually they sang a better than average version of "The Lady is a Tramp" and "Volare." Mixed in with the vocals, they performed a few skits and told some very old and worn jokes.

"Hey Dean" Dad approached the stage following the performance. "Did you hear about the Priest, the Minister, and the Rabbi who were gambling?"

"Dean" shook his head, "No, I haven't heard that one." Politely he listened though he was probably eager to leave the theater for a few hours of rest and relaxation before the evening show. Dad continued, "A Priest, a minister, and a Rabbi were playing poker when the police raided the game."

"Turning to the Priest, the officer said "Father Murphy were you gambling?"

Under his breath the Father whispered "Forgive me Lord for what I am about to do. 'No officer, I was not gambling'."

The officer turned to the Minister. "Pastor Johnson, were you gambling?" He looked to the heavens then said, "No officer, I was not gambling."

Turning to the Rabbi, the officer asked, "Rabbi Goldstein were you gambling?" At this point Dad shrugged his shoulders and in as close as he could come to a Yiddish accent said, "So who was I gambling with?"

Dean chortled. "Hey, I think I will use that in my show."

And with that, Dad was back in show business.

Each day forty-seven passenger buses rolled in to Branson and visitors with canes, walkers, wheelchairs, hearing aids, and most likely an inordinate number of replaced body parts, gingerly climbed down the bus steps to attend the variety of shows featuring impersonators, B-stars, and variety acts.

Dad was upbeat about every show during our stay. It made no difference who or what we booked. He relished them all while Mom, in a fog, followed along with a blank smile. Every day we attended an afternoon show and an evening show.

Between the shows we partook of cookie cutter local restaurants. Most of the eating facilities boasted of comfort food. One day we chose a nondescript family style coffee shop that was crowded with customers. We entered the restaurant and joined the crowd of elderly tourists waiting for a table. In typical form, Dad surveyed the area for an audience while we waited. Right and left he found cheerful seniors with whom to strike up a conversation. He zeroed in on an octogenarian wearing suspenders that held up baggy jeans and he proceeded to tell a joke. At the end of the joke the old man snickered "Since you've given me a laugh, I want to give your wife something. Here is a dime-in-pin for her."

And then he handed Mom a safety pin with a dime attached. A small hole had been drilled through the dime and a jump ring secured the coin to the pin. I saw Dad's eyes light up. I could see his mind working overtime. The invention of the light bulb could not have generated a greater spark for Thomas Edison than the look on Dad's face.

When we arrived back home Dad made it his mission to manufacture "dime-in-pins." He shopped local craft stores studying various safety pin sizes, finishes, and quality. He made a trip to the bank just to acquire rolls of dimes. He settled on large gold safety pins, purchased dozens of jump rings, and spent afternoons in the garage drilling holes in the dimes.

From then on he never left home without a few dime-in-pins in his pocket. He gifted pins like others offer breath mints or gum. Over the years he bestowed these on friends and strangers alike. Just as he sought in the past, his reward for the pin was a laugh or a smile. Exiting a restaurant now took longer than ordering and eating an entire meal as Dad went table to table working the room and giving out pins.

A homemade card found a few years ago was a sample of what he got in return. "Mr. Schultz, you are #1- the best- Your jokes are #1." Inside was a typed message. "Thank you for the Dime and Pin. (Everyone asks me about it)." It was signed, "Fondly, JoAnn, Nurse Practitioner." And a postscript-"Thanks for the candy bar, also."

43

"The Times They Are a-Changin"

Dad was in his mid eighties and still driving around town in his beloved Camry shopping for tchotchkes and taking Mom out to lunch. Ruby's Diner was a favorite restaurant where they enjoyed lunch every couple of weeks. It was not just the food, but Dad had become friendly with one of the young waiters. During each visit, after being seated, he surveyed the room looking for his favorite server. If he saw the young Black man he would call him over "Hi Jimmy, how's school going?" He really did care. During one conversation Jimmy mentioned he was in a band and they were playing a gig downtown. "Hey, would you want to come see me perform?" the teen asked. Mom and Dad, easily fifty plus years older than anyone else in the audience at the bar, watched their favorite waiter make his musical debut. The loud unfamiliar genre meant nothing to Mom or Dad but the young man's smile when he spotted them was worth the effort.

For a number of years my Saturday afternoon outings included just Mom and me. In my daydreams they would be reminiscent of the scores of afternoons of my youth when we had shared shopping, chatting, and intimate lunches. But these excursions were nothing like the past. Mom was no longer leading me. I was in the lead now.

At that time Dad was Mom's sole caregiver. "I can take care of Mom. I don't need anyone else staying here." Mom was still able to talk, eat by herself, and with some assistance, dress and take care of herself. My excursions served to give Dad a few hours of much needed respite. He lovingly did his best, though many times his frustration would get the best of him. He would yell at Mom for her missteps though she never understood his anger. I encouraged him to do something, anything, or nothing, during the few hours I took her on an outing.

I held Mom's arm, assisting her into the car and we drove to the mall each week. Her conversation on the way was one of constant repetition. "Look at the houses there. They all look alike. How would you know where you lived?" Over and over, like a broken record, she repeated this both to and from the mall. We walked from the parking lot past the store windows where I tried to stimulate a conversation without much success. At Nordstrom's we lined up at the cafe, ordered the same salad as the previous week and the week before, and nodded in familiarity to the wait staff.

After lunch, we browsed the store with no plan other than to clock some time. "Do you think all these people came across the border?" Mom, obviously bewildered, commented observing African American shoppers. Sometimes she would innocently point to an obese person, "Look at him. He is so big." Her filters were non-existent though she maintained a sweetness. Some time during each afternoon together, she simply commented, "It's a different world." That was an understatement. Every so often my eyes welled up and my heart ached when she said, "I don't know what I am doing. I am so confused." I could feel her fear during those moments. Then it was my job to reassure her and provide calm.

In hopes that Dad would enjoy a change of scenery I offered an invitation. "Hi Dad, how about if you and Mom come up to dinner this weekend?" "H-m-m-m, I don't know. I have to ask my social director," he answered as he turned to Mom, in denial of the disconnected look on her face. Though Dad's eyes were a clear baby blue, he chose not to see what was right in front of him.

In time Dad was happy to join Mom and me on our weekly Saturday afternoon excursions. From that point on our route and itinerary changed. Instead of browsing through the mall, Dad preferred a car ride down memory lane, always with lunch. He did all the talking while Mom just stared, literally going along for the ride.

I was the escort, chauffeur, cheerleader, and untrained caregiver. It gave me pleasure to spend the afternoon with Mom and Dad, though the decline of their health was a thousand volt shock each week, and a depressing one. I put Mom's jacket on her and walked her to the car, carefully helping her to the back seat. Dad orchestrated our adventure from the front seat after he struggled to lift his weakened legs in to the passenger side. Mom looked out the window, unaware of where we were going. Her mind appeared to be a blank slate though I wondered if she had any coherent thoughts trapped inside her broken body.

Dad always had a plan for the day. "Suzi-belle, let's drive to National City. I want to look at what's happened to the building we owned a few years ago. I wanna see how it has been developed. Okay?" As we cruised through different areas of the city Dad knew well from his childhood, he commented, "See that lot over there? It used to be an auto repair shop and over there was a restaurant — though not a very good one." He was my tour guide bringing alive the history of the city he loved for over eight decades. His mind was still sharp as he noticed new construction or a property that had been redesigned. And Mom just stared.

Other Saturdays we headed to one of the many Indian Casinos in San Diego county for lunch. As we entered the casino Dad's sparkle returned. He had no desire to play the slots but relished looking at the high-tech machines so different than the ones his brother repaired. He watched patrons enthusiastically slide plastic cards uploaded with money in to the slot machines. It was obvious he missed old sounds of a jackpot being hit: *b-r-r-r-ing, b-r-r-ing,* when the lights blinked, the sirens sounded, and the *c-l-ang, c-l-ang* of coins dropping in the tray beneath. "Will ya take a look at that? Brother Jack wouldn't believe this," he marveled. The technology was beyond his comprehension. And Mom just stared.

One particular Saturday we took a ride to Imperial Beach where Dad had owned a beachfront piece of land. He had decided at his age he didn't have the energy to build on the land and sold it as vacant, very valuable, real estate. Dad was extremely chatty and vivacious. After the half hour ride south he directed me to the alley running parallel to the ocean. I pulled the car off to the side and shifted into park. He opened the car door with eyes wide open as he moved his head slowly up to see the third story of the recently erected modern style condominiums. "Hey, take a look at that. What a terrific job they did building this. If I was younger I would have done the same thing. Okay, how about some lunch?" Satisfied with the work by current owners of his property, off we went.

We stopped at a busy sandwich shop in Coronado on the way back and ordered turkey sandwiches. Mom still knew how to eat, chew, and swallow so our lunch was without mishaps. But with each outing it became apparent that these skills were diminishing. I reminded myself, *Enjoy the day. Enjoy the moment. Be thankful for what she can do.* The afternoon had been successful, meaning there were no falls and no bathroom accidents. Mom sat quietly in the car and at lunch, occasionally mumbling something neither Dad nor I could understand. The mission of the Saturday outing had now changed. It provided a few hours for Dad to cruise through the past and present in the city he loved and escape from reality.

I was in a hurry one afternoon, thinking about getting on the freeway towards home before traffic increased and to prepare for a Saturday night out with Chuck and friends. As I rounded the corner onto Point Loma Avenue where Mom and Dad lived, I glanced in my rearview mirror. It was late in the day. The California sun was setting in the west shining through the back window of my car, obscuring my vision. "Uh oh" I mumbled under my breath. I tensed as the red flashing lights of a police car overtook the sun's glare and the black and white pulled up behind me. My mind whirled as I reviewed the last mile. *Did I go though a red light? Did I cut someone off?* I had no time to dwell and slowly pulled over to the curb. I stopped and put the car in park and hesitantly rolled down the window. I was anxious, like a small child sure I was going to be lectured for running in the street again.

The young man in uniform sidled up to my window. "Hello Ma'am. Did you realize there was a stop sign and you didn't make a complete stop?" "Why no Officer," I timidly replied. *Actually I did know. This was standard operating procedure - a 'California Stop' - really a slow roll through the red STOP sign and an inching forward.* I was right around the corner in this upper-middle class neighborhood and had never, in all the years of driving this route on the same streets to the house on the hill, observed a policeman. "I am sorry Officer. I am just taking my parents back home after spending the afternoon with them." Mom sat in the backseat unaware of my discomfort - that I felt like a deer in the headlights.

Dad put on his million-dollar smile and before the officer continued, he chimed in, "Officer, have you ever been to the Miramar Air Show? My daughter is in charge of it."

Yes, I was Marketing Director at Marine Corps Air Station Miramar. But out of the 3000 plus employees who worked on the world class Air Show, the importance of my position ranked close to the bottom. No, I did not fly above the 100,000 attendees in a fighter jet demonstration. No, I did not jump from a plane with an American flag waving behind me as I glided to the ground. No, I did not coordinate the Marines or Sailors who recruited new prospects with flashy exhibits. No, I did not even assist in the set-up or tear-down of the bleachers. I merely worked to market the event through all forms of media and spent a good share of the year at a desk job seeking out sponsorship. I loved my job, but being "in charge" was more than an exaggeration.

Dad continued "She can get you good tickets if you want some." *What? Employees had no special discounts or freebies.* But Dad was not above bribery. "It's a terrific show and she can get you in the VIP area. You can take your family. How many tickets would you like?" I was speechless. I tried to make myself as small as possible. How would Dad look, an octogenarian, handcuffed in the back of the police car on his way to jail? The charges were obvious-trying to bribe an officer of the law!

The policeman hesitated. I could feel his dilemma. He made a deep sigh as I held my breath wondering what would happen next. Finally, this kind upholder of the law tried to contain his smile. He realized getting this criminal off the street was not in the best interest of serving the community. "Okay, I'm just going to warn you. Don't do it again. Make a complete stop at every stop sign." "Yes sir, thank you, I will" I responded meekly. Dad continued talking, never missing a beat, as I inched away slowly from the curb.

It was another outing on this roller coaster with my aging parents. Dad's humor and Mom's pleasant manner were still evident though most other characteristics of Mom and Dad's personalities were gone.

I reviewed the day as I drove home. There was a sense of comedy alongside the tragedy. Dad was still there to support me, what ever gimmick it took, even if it involved buying off a police officer with a few free event tickets.

*Dad & me at his 90th
birthday celebration*

44

"Love You Baby"

There was no more pretending. The family was forced to acknowledge both Mom's and Dad's decline. For decades the family's closeness had provided some comfort to me, like soaking in a soothing bath of steaming hot water. In a short time the steam dissipates, the calming weightlessness of water cools to warm, then cold. But more hot water couldn't be added. We simply had to get out and face the cold truth.

We had rationalized and made excuses for Mom. "She must have taken too much medicine. It must be a UTI that is making her incoherent. It's natural to forget things as you age." We had finally taken her to a doctor who administered a test to measure cognitive impairment. Our fears were realized. The doctor confirmed Mom had moderate memory loss and it would get worse. *How could we fix this? Wasn't there a cure? It seemed impossible that there was no bandaid, no magic pill, no 'snake oil', no way to reverse the inevitable.* Mom was prescribed medication with the goal to slowing the progression of her disease. Sadly, it was the best and only option.

Dad's wish to take care of her had worn him down and compromised his own health. He was no longer able to perform routine daily tasks for both of them. They needed full-time caregivers. His physical body had weakened and his interests in the world had narrowed. Even our weekly excursions were now a thing of the past.

Caregivers were hired for the day shift and overnight. Help was necessary round the clock, seven days a week, to assist with basic needs: getting dressed, showering, going to the bathroom.

"Don't bother to visit me in the nursing home," Dad joked. "I'll just tell everyone that I asked you to honk the horn when you drive by. That way every time I hear a horn honk I can brag to everyone, 'There my kids are. They come by all the time.'"

Truthfully, his wishes were the opposite. He let the family know "Mom and I want to stay home, in our own house, forever."

At the age of ninety Dad presented me with a large brown envelope during my visit. "Suzi-belle, keep this is a safe place," he directed with no further explanation. When I arrived home I reached into the envelope and retrieved a copy of his Advanced Directive. He had checked the box *"I do not want my life prolonged..."* Attached to the formal sheet of instructions was a scrap of paper with his easily recognizable scribble. *"Suzi-belle, here is a copy of the Advanced Directive for your file. Remember, get a second opinion. You're not a doctor. Love Pop."*

In April 2012 I headed to an intimate 65th birthday lunch I was hosting for a beloved friend at a "proper" English Tearoom. Our small group of friends were dressed in what we considered tearoom clothes, wearing fascinators purchased specifically to be in vogue with what we had read cultured British women wore. We were escorted to a table covered with daintily embroidered edging on a delicate white cloth.

All our years of friendship prompted endless chatter. We commiserated about years flying by, getting old, and being old. The consensus among these long-time friends was the same.

We had gone from idealistic young women to being involved mothers and now we were observing our creations. In our minds, though not our bodies, we were still at the beginning - busy raising children. With the last sips of tea and bites of scones we shared cute stories about our grandchildren.

I had rearranged the timing of my usual Saturday outing with Mom and Dad. I planned my visit to immediately follow this celebration of friendships. The group birthday gift had been opened when my cell phone rang. I saw my sister's name on the face of the phone. I was immediately catapulted away from the tearoom and back to the present. "Hi Suzi," Judy's voice was anxious. "We've taken Dad to Urgent Care at UCSD. He's confused and lethargic and needs to be checked out." An ominous fear ran through my body. "I will meet you there."

Thoughts coursed through my mind as I drove the twenty minutes to the hospital. *Please don't make this the end. Let him get over this hurdle. I am not ready to say good-bye.* I parked as quickly as possible and entered Urgent Care, a place that always exposed my nerves. "I'm here to see my dad, Sol Schultz. Can you please buzz me in?" I impatiently asked the receptionist. Entering his room, Dad glanced up at me, his blue eyes at half-mast. "Hi baby," he murmured. "How you feeling Poppy?" I questioned. "Not too good right now," he whispered. I held his hand and kissed his forehead as the nurse entered to take vitals and inform us of tests being ordered.

Hours later he was diagnosed with a urinary tract infection. Due to his advanced age of 93, he was admitted to a hospital room until the infection could be gotten under control. He uttered in a weak voice, "Love you baby" as I left for the evening. During my visits throughout the following week I saw little improvement.

Dad's star was fading, his usual sparkle dimming. He spiraled down a bit each day and was moved to ICU where his condition had been compromised with MRSA, a bacterial staph infection. When informed by a hospice worker days later that he had limited time left on earth, he was transferred where he wanted to be. He came home to his beloved Point Loma bedroom surrounded by family pictures and loved ones. The hospice nurse checked in regularly, joining the twenty-four hour caregivers. He seemed to sink further with each visit. On April 16, 2012, I received a phone call "Signs are evident that the end is coming soon - in just a few hours," the nurse's soft voice resonated.

We arrived in time to sit at his bedside and hold the hand of a good man, a good father, a man who lived a good and full life and had given me the gift of life. His breathing became irregular, then he gasped and all was quiet.

I kissed his cheek and silently thanked him. I was grateful that I had been blessed with Dad's unfailing love and support. I had inherited a bit of his drive, though my creativity and zeal for life hardly equaled his. I certainly hadn't been gifted with his sense of humor or wit, just his thick thighs. He was unique. He was one of a kind. He was my dad.

Mom and Dad had always been there to catch me when I failed, to show pride in my successes. They had been role models for parenting. Mom's mind had failed years prior. Now Dad was gone physically, though his stories, his colorful life, and his spirit, lived on.

45

Butterfly Wings

The months following Dad's passing felt like a raw and open wound. I missed his "Hi Baby," his smile, the bits of humor he displayed to the end. Sadness hit me at various times of the day, whenever my mind was unoccupied with mundane daily tasks. I flashed on Dad's smile when I stopped at a red light. I was jolted by the loss when I stepped out of bed each morning. Sorrow took over my thoughts when I least expected it.

Mom's heart was still beating, though she was residing in a casing of her stiffened body. I continued to visit her each week, hoping on some level she knew I was there. If not, I knew I was there.

Judy and Ed continued to check in with the caregivers handling the multitude of questions and problems that were endless. Between organizing medication, doctor's appointments and paying the bills, it was a huge responsibility. I was most appreciative.

The purpose of my weekly visit was still self-serving. I wanted the caregivers to know that Mom was loved and I, selfishly, just wanted her there. I wasn't ready to be an orphan. But my visits were shorter, the conversation with Mom non-existent. The caregivers would tell me what they thought I'd like to hear so we continued to play this game for months.

I had prayed that Dad would pass away before Mom for I believed he couldn't or wouldn't have wanted to live without her. It made no difference to him what her physical or mental state was. He just wanted her there in bed next to him each night. It had been a blessing that he passed on while Mom's body still graced the earth.

I had learned to insulate myself from the anguish of her condition. Her final words to me more than a year prior were, "You look lovely," one day when I walked in the kitchen. She looked directly at me and clearly spoke these treasured words between incoherent babbling. They comforted me and I played them over and over in my mind. That is where I chose to live; in the last recognizable verbal interaction with Mom.

Months passed until her contracted, shrunken body could fight no more. She passed away on February 3, 2013, ten months after Dad. Now they would again be together to continue their seventy-six year love story.

It was shortly after Mom died that I spent one of many afternoons in my backyard. The sun was directly overhead and as spring was approaching, the shrubs and flowers were coming alive. Purple African Daisies covered the bank and honey bees swarmed among the tiny flowers of the Red Apple ground cover. The beams of light from the sun shone directly on our black-bottom pool and the water sparkled like the stars in the clear night sky. It was a mindless afternoon, void of thoughts.

I sat on the rattan sofa with my granddog, Fonzie, resting his head on my lap. His soft black furry body occasionally jerked as he most likely was dreaming of lizards and rabbits to chase. The sky was a clear blue, not a cloud in view. The vivid contrast of the sky against the various shades of green created a jagged skyline of tall pines and the shorter magnolia tree with one huge white bloom. *How could there be so many shades of green?* I daydreamed, drifting to mindless thoughts of the number of 'greens' in the largest box of Crayolas.

Something caught my eye. It flickered in waves dancing from the right side of the yard to the left. It was a magnificent performance by a butterfly, the color of a hundred watt light bulb. Its bright yellow wings fluttered against the tapestry behind the pool. The butterfly's graceful movements lasted a mere thirty seconds and then it disappeared. Yet in that time I felt the presence of Mom. It was a sign - the bright light of her existence that would continue to remain in my memory and heart.

I searched the internet for the meaning of a yellow butterfly. I was surprised that there were many legends, superstitions, and folklore associated with its presence. I have chosen to believe the following:

"A yellow butterfly represents joy and creativity. A yellow butterfly flying around you brings happiness and prosperity. Seeing one also means that something fun and exciting is on its way."

When I least expect it, when daydreams are just daydreams, a yellow butterfly will cross my path. Immediately a sense of calm will come over me, a sense of happiness, that all is right in my world, and I feel the essence of Mom.

Dad's Words of Wisdom

Take your good time with you.

Just do it (long before this was the Nike motto)!

Make a decision! If it's the wrong one, make another one.

If you haven't used it in six months, dump it!

Make it a fair deal. Don't be greedy.

There's always room for one more.

Enough is enough.

Fair is fair.

Did you hear the one about…?

I love you, Baby.

Mom's Words of Wisdom

Look at the moon and remember that we are looking at the same moon. So wherever you are we are close together.

Life is a great equalizer; sometimes you are up and sometimes you are down.

I'm not asking for myself.

Save it for the important things.

If it can be replaced by money, don't worry about it.

Adversity builds character.

Aren't you lucky?

Aren't we lucky?

Post Script: Dad's Humor

Dad wrote this tongue in cheek story regarding taxes that was published for the Aztec literary magazine.

An Education is a Wonderful Thing

So the chief is lookin' at me an' sayin', "Joe, I wanna buy a football team," he sez just like that.

"Boss," I sez, sez I, "Boss, you are of a certainty out of your cranium. I have not seen a single lucre made on the inflated porter game yet except the gees that run the outfits."

He jest looks at me sorrowful like an' he sez quietly, "Joe," he sez, "Have you ever heard of income tax?"

"Oh" I sez. "No, but what has carpet nails to do with football?"

"My goodness me, you are very dumb," he sez. (He is the only chap that can call me that cause he got a diploma from grammar school an' is very edjucated. He also insists us boys go to night school to get better edjucated since he sez an edjucation is a wonderful thing an' we are all goin' to school.) "Income tax is----is----well---you see, if you make big dough, Uncle Samuel wants a cut," he finishes explainin'.

"Listen Boss," I sez madlike, "No Uncle or no other guy's musclin' in on our dough. I gets the boys an' we works dis (excites me, this) gee over."

"Tck,tck," sez the boss, "Uncle Samuel ain't nobody."

"That's right, Boss," I sez, happy to see the boss does not fear anyone and still considers hisself tops in our racket, which I have not aforehand said is "Winkum Blinkum Beer, the Beer with a Cheer" made in U.S.A. America.

"Naw," he sez at me, "Uncle Samuel is the whole gov't, the whole U.S.A."

Dear me, I sez to myself, the boys will have to work very hard for this job, an' I asks the boss if we can hire a couple more fellows to help us since he has not had such a big job before, not even during prohibition.

"Shut up," snaps the boss, "Lemme tell you about this."

An' he does. He tells me how he has to shell out every year on accounta our wonderful beverage makes the hard silver stuff roll into our bank books and I do not mean that he saves tinfoil. I do not quite understand why if he loses money this Sammie guy takes less, be he (the boss, not Sammie) tells me that it is very legal. An' it only goes to show that he (this Sammie guy) is a very square shooter, as the boss sez. But the boss sez he has too much dough, an' if he gets a football club the dough will diminish (which means, get less) an' then he does not come in the upper bracket an' he really makes dough, which is very mixed up to me.

"Go, Joe," he sez, "an' buy me a nice little football team to go with a college, which you will buy very nicely an' when you are ready I will come an' I want a big band to meet me at the depo (which is train station, I found out) in uniforms an' everthing."

So he is givin' me A.W.O.L. which means in the army "Take off a week or longer" an' here I am on my way in a bus I am drivin' which is a present from some of the boys who heard we needed a football coach. So now I am drivin' this bus (football coach) down the main drag of town just before I shoves off for some place called South Bend which I understand has a football team an' a bus (football coach) named after a football player called one of the horsemen or somethin', so I decide our coach's name will be C-biskit which is a very good horse.

Well, who should I run into (verbally) but "Slapsie" Hapsie who is an ex-pug an' a little bit on the punchy side. In fact, it is very dangerous to ring a bell near him as he will toss punches for a few seconds an' then flop (fall, excuse me) on his back which he is used to on accounta his wonderful ability to take a dive in the ring. So I am beeping the horn an' he is smiling an' sayin' who do I want, an' I am telling him my business, an' I sez can you play an' he pulls out a handful of clippings that tells how good he was in high school an' how he was to make All-American in collitch if he went out but he does not go to collitch. (I know he has not his citizenship papers yet so he could not make All-American legally.) An' he tells me how onc't he seen a movin' picture show where a gangster (which word I do not like) hired a bunch of wrestlers an' boxers to play football for a college he owns an' I sez no we will not do just that as the boss want only edjucated men in college an' on his football team, but I will take you anyway. So we leave.

On our way to South Bend I decide to go to Pineville Univ. in Pineville, Mont. Which has a school, Pineville U., which I have said before. I understand it is for sale so I am arriving there one beautiful day an' look the campus (joint) over. I decide it is O.K. and will be ours soon, so I ambles up to the prexy (which means president) an' sez, "Joe Hunk," I sez, "I wish to buy your school" an' he's sayin' "Oke," an' so I gives him a blank check an' tells him, "O.K. Write your own ticket," I sez an' he puts in ten G's which I figgers is cheap.

Then I sez, how about a football team, an' he sez, yes, they have one and what is more they have a wonderful schedule, but they lose much money each game as there is many hurt players after each game. So I feel good as I have spent ten G's and I sez, how many students here, an' he sez 239, an' 28 football players, so I orders 239 uniforms for the band I was to start an' also I orders instruments an' this takes plenty of dough but I still have too much left, so I raises the pay of all the fackulties (which means teachers) an' everything is O.K. an' I looks over the football team which looks very, very no good an' speaks to the coach. (I am sorry. I mistook a football coach. It is not a bus an' I shall return the bus immediately an' tell the peaceful citizens who gave it to me to return it where they got it, an', "Coach," I sez, "I unnerstand you got a good schedule."

He sez, yes, but they have not a good team, so I asks him can he get a good team? He sez for five G's he can put some good football players in school, so I hands him a check for five G's an' he passes out like a lite. I also sez, order new equipment for the team, jest like that. Also I asks if "Slapsie" Hapsie can play on the team an' again he breaks down an' cries an' sez "*The* Slapsie Hapsie?" "Yes," sez I.

"Oh, he sez, "We will not use his real name, but will use an alias." I think this is very considerate of him, as "Slapsie" is not a very good fighter in his day, and does not draw even flies when he fights an' he is very sensitive about this an' is in doldrums for weeks at a time, so the chance to change his name is very well taken by him.

Immediately, one week after, I go out to watch football practice an' the coach is all grins an' he tells me that "Slapsie," whose name is now Robert Grantville, is goin' like a house afire an' is what you call a three threater which means that he can kick and/or pass, and/or run very good or do all three I think.

I decide it is time to get the boss down as we play Hahvahd the nex' week. So I wires him an' he comes on the streamline train in a special rush an' he is grinnin' from eat to ear at the size of the band an' he is very happy. In fact, he is thinkin' of getting' Paul Whiteman to lead it an' sends him a wire offerin' much do-re-mi, but P.W. is tied up with a contract an' cannot break it so anyway it is O.K.

An' now our football. We are playin' Hahvahd an' winnin' which is considered the major upset of the day an' nex' week when we play Yale we are winnin' again an' we are hailed as Flower Bowl threats which means that if we win some more games we play on Jan. 1 some other team in Calif. Or Pasadena, the Flower Bowl, an' this I unnerstand is very good for a team but I am very worried as the tickets for our game wit Dornmouth is a sellout already an' we are supposed to make good dough which will not please the boss.

I forgot to tell about why we have such a good football schedule which includes such as Hahvahd, Yale, Dornmouth, Princetown, Northsouthern, Minnesoda, Perdue, Wahington, Pittsburgh, an' Carnegie Teck. When we gets such top teams? Well it seems as if the (the big teams) wants what they calls a "breather" game which means they wants a cinch game to be sure an' win an' since P.U. never wins a game in many years O.K. they signs us up before the season an' it is by written contract too as a verbal contract ain't worth the paper it's written on!

So we are upsetting the two big teams all ready an' then we smash Dornmouth with "Slapsie" makin' 17 points himself an' bein' hailed as All-American.

Well, we beat all the rest of the teams an' we get much publicity an' the crowd pours in an' so does the dough, much to my disgust, but we build new buildings an' we have a marble swimmin' pool built an' new tennis courts an' the boss is givin' each football player a new automobile an' we has a great big hunnert foot neon sign on the school which says "Winkum Blinkum Beer is the Best" an' still we got dough left which the boss says give to charity an' I does an' he is known as a humanitarian or sompin'! Well anyhow!

We reach our last game against Carnagie Teck. An' they are leadin' the game 3 to 0 an' just a few minutes to go. Now, it seems as if this school is very smart an' they have a very good reputation of bein' smart an' the boss says to the team to watch out for sompin' funny as an edjacation (excue me edj-education) is a wonderful thing an' a collitch with such a record as Carnagie Teck is likely to have very smart members so watch out. AN' we are! 95,000 people here, too!

"Slapsie" makes many long runs but when we gets near the goal we cannot score as the officials are always interruptin' our chanctes an' so we are behin' 3 to 0.

Seconds to go an we are on our own 5 yard line, as due to penalties for roughness, an' other things.

We are very blue. NO Flower Bowl. No nothin'!

An' then it happens—with one play to go "Slapsie" breaks loose an' heads for the goal line, which is, I understand, some 95 yards away an' no one near him! We are cheerin' an' I am singin' "Flower Bowl here we come" an' then--

Some one on the Carnagie bench rings a bell as "Slapsie" is about to cross the goal line an' he stops an' I yealls "go on" as the other team is catchin' up an' he licks his lips an' the bell is rung again an' "Slapsie" see these guys comin' an' he drops the ball an' starts sparrin' the air with his fists an' then he passes out like a lite an' the other team gets the ball on the one yard line an' the gun sounds to end the game an' we lose 3 to 0 an' I am sore.

I walks over to the boss an' say that I am goin' to get the ringer an' the boss sez smilin:

"Of course you will not. These collitch lads are too smart for us an' they are findin' out about "Slapsie" but as collitch lads are gents they do not get mad but think up a better way to beat us an' I am not angry at all. An' anyway my brewery is blowing up the other night an' the gov't an' Uncle Samuel has offered to give me W.P.A.* to rebuild an' this is very nice an' so I am giving them the school an' everything an' I shall never again try to chisel on the gov't or Uncle Samuel again an' I will pay my income tax. They sure were smart to ring that bell, these collitch boys. Tck, tck. An edjucation is a wonderful thing.

* Founded in 1935 by Franklin D. Roosevelt: The Works Progress Administration was the largest and most ambitious American New Deal agency, employing millions of people to carry out public works projects, including the construction of public buildings and roads. (Wikipedia.org)

Mother

A two character scene in the living room of the Mepplewhites

Mrs H: A divorcee

Laura Mae: Her daughter 17 who is a senior in high school

Mrs. H: Looks out the window, very anxious, until she sees a car drive up and Laura Mae gets out. Mrs. H sits herself on the edge of the overstuffed chair as Laura Mae enters.

Mrs. H: Grim face, loud voice. When I said be home at 12 o'clock I did NOT mean 12 o'clock noon. Today.

LM: I stayed at Becky Lee's house.

Mrs. H: Don't lie to me young lady. I called Mrs. Lee and she thought Becky was staying with you in a sleepover.

LM: MOTHER! You did what? You called Mrs. Lee? What are you, an FBI agent or with the Gestapo?

Mrs. H: Don't lie to me Miss. You were with that bum Rambo.

LM: MOTHER. His name is Randolph. He is going to be a rock musician and be rich.

Mrs. H: Ha. The way he dresses he could be. When he took you to the Junior Prom his rented tux was size 46 — My Gawd, he's only a skinny 36.

LM: Big clothes are in style.

Mrs. H:--and that hair (shakes her head).

LM: All the top rock stars wear a ponytail.

Mrs. H: His must be a horsetail. It hangs below his ass.

LM: MOTHER!

Mrs. H: And his tux — with tennis shoes — and no socks!

LM: Those Reeboks cost $149.

Mrs. H: And how many times has he been picked up by the police for an IUD?

LM: MOTHER. That's a DUI, driving under the influence. Besides he wasn't guilty.

Mrs. H: Only because his father is on the District Attorney's staff.

LM: I'll be glad when this semester is over and I graduate. I won't have to listen to your sneaky-spy accusations. Then when I go to college, I'm going to live with Daddy.

Mrs. H: Wonderful. Your stepmother is only two years older than you. She and your father can double date with you and Rambo.

LM: (bursting into tears) I don't have to listen to this. I'm going to my room. (Exits)

Phone rings-

Mrs. H: Hello. Oh yes Mrs. Lee. I sure did. She'll think twice before lying to me again. Punishment? You better believe it. No driving for two weeks. I'll take her to school. In at 10 PM every weekend for the next two weeks. (Hesitates) Oh, I forgot Becky Lee is having her party next week. Well, okay, one week of punishment. Oh, yes, I'm glad you reminded me of our week of volunteer work. She'll have to drive herself to school — but I'll warn her. She is not getting off too easy next time it happens. (Silence) What was that? Neiman-Marcus is having a showing of Senior Prom outfits Saturday? Of course we'll go. And by the way why don't we take the girls to lunch first — they would like that.

The Ark

Scene: On the deck of the ARK, built by Mr. Noah, a man about six hundred years old is talking (listening) to his wife.

N. I don't want to talk about it.

W. I do.

N. I don't want to talk about it.

W. You and your big ideas.

N. I am going to take a nap.

W. "Look dear" you said. "We'll take a vacation cruise. The whole family. Our three boys and their wives." And like a fool, I listened.

N. I'm going to take a nap.

W. "Fine" I said. "I'll pick something for deck wear and dinner." And what have we got? Forty days and forty nites of rain. Not one day have I had my sunsuit on! I've been cooped up like a chicken in the cabin. And speaking of chickens, I thought they were for food but no, you had some other idea about them, and the cattle, not even fresh milk! You know what Noah? I've had it up to here. (Hand over her head). I want to go home. This stinks.

N. I don't know exactly where we are.

W. What do you mean?

N. My chief navigator did not tell me exactly where our ports were.

W. Are you crazy? Or are you drunk? I know you brought two of everything on board but I only see one keg of wine left.

N. I sent a dove out this morning and he came back with a twig.

W. Wonderful. Now send a monkey out and maybe we will have bananas to eat. I've put up with you for over 500 years but this takes the cake. If it wasn't for the children I'd get a divorce. I shouldn't have married you if you were the last man on earth.

N. But, dear, when we dock I will be.

W. I don't want to talk about it.

Paying it Forward

After they passed away, I endeavored to find a way to honor my parents. Since they had met, courted, danced, studied, and acted together at San Diego State University, I decided to share the financial benefit I was fortunate to have inherited from them by creating a scholarship in their name. I believe this will pay tribute to the place where they began their life together and will pass on the generosity they demonstrated without fanfare throughout their marriage.

As stated on the San Diego State University website, "SDSU Guardian Scholars Program is a holistic support program committed to serving students who identify as current or former foster youth, wards of the court, under legal guardianship or unaccompanied homeless youth by supporting their transition to, through and beyond San Diego State University."

The **Sol and Charlotte Schultz Scholarship** is given each year to students accepted in this program who major either in Education or Business and/or are involved in some type of community service.

I know that Mom and Dad would be proud of these students who rise above their past and overcome obstacles to succeed.

This is a small part of my parent's legacy and the many gifts that will live on in their memory.

Acknowledgments

I never imagined that my story would take eight years to write. In truth it was a lonely but cathartic endeavor. When I thought I couldn't read the umpteenth draft, I would make myself start at the beginning once again and change the wording, rewrite paragraphs, delete excess, and add a tidbit that had somehow just risen to the forefront of my brain. I finally got to the point where I felt Dad's spirited exclamation, 'Enough is Enough.'

On Dad's 80th birthday I presented him with a scrapbook. He had a love of writing and I hoped this would encourage him to fill the empty book. On each page I had attached a sheet of legal paper with a title at the top. I was hoping he would write his history on the lined paper. I was eager for memories of his childhood, his college days, meeting Mom, and life as he viewed it when my sister and I were growing up. After he passed away thirteen years later I came across the scrapbook. It became my gift since Dad had actually completed many pages with stories in his own handwriting. Many of his actual words are included in this book and this was just the prompt I needed to begin my memoir.

I got great boosts of confidence out of classes at San Diego Writers, Ink. Thanks to my Read and Critique classmates who helped me grow from feeling too embarrassed to read a few pages aloud, to looking forward to exposing my words and hearing their praise as well as their constructive suggestions. It took a while to feel secure enough to share my happy, simple, mundane story that lacked the dramatic circumstances everyone else seemed to have in their past. Thank you Kathy, my first friend to read the entire manuscript and who encouraged me to keep going.

My sister, Huki, was valuable in recalling childhood events. In many instances I relied on her to confirm or provide details of an event.

My amazing children, Josh and Lindsay, both have successful careers and busy lives. Lindsay offered to read a final draft of which I am most appreciative. Her comments and edits were invaluable. She made me see this project with fresh eyes, sensitive to family events from her insider's viewpoint.

Chuck, my husband and love, has been by my side for over fifty years. He was a reader of one of the first drafts and one of the last drafts. I hope I have portrayed his strength, stability, and conviction. I am thankful that he is so organized, handles the important things, most of the household tasks, and doesn't grumble when I am at the computer for hours on end. Most of all, I appreciate that he wakes up with a smile every single day. He is my rock.

At 74, I consider old age a gift! Hey, plenty of people don't make it this far. And I am here in one piece, a bit shop worn, but still realizing my good fortune on a daily basis. Chuck, Josh and his wife, Katherine, Lindsay and husband, Mike, my perfect grandchildren, Lucy, Charlie, and Max, and my granddog, Fonzie, give me all the reasons I need to count my good fortune every day.

Chuck and I have raised wonderful, kind adults who are bright, competent, contributing citizens of the world.

That is my greatest accomplishment. I am proud….but I still have a ways to go and things I want to achieve. In Dad's words, " I'm on third base..."

Three Generations:
Front Row: Marc, Mom, Dad, Me, Josh
Back Row: Judy, Derek, Ed, Lindsay, Chuck

Made in the USA
Las Vegas, NV
08 May 2021

22714123R00138